ECCE HOMO

ECCE HOMO

FRIEDRICH NIETZSCHE

SIRIUS

SIRIUS

This edition published in 2024 by Sirius Publishing, a division of
Arcturus Publishing Limited,
26/27 Bickels Yard, 151–153 Bermondsey Street,
London SE1 3HA

ISBN: 978-1-3988-3640-2
AD006327UK

Printed in China

Contents

Introduction

Friedrich Nietzsche wrote his last book and literary autobiography *Why I Am So Wise* in 1888; it was finally published in 1908 under the title *Ecce Homo* and subtitled *How we become what we are*, which is nothing but the old Delphic saying 'Know thyself'. This became one of his most compelling messages.

Born on 15 October 1844 in the small German village of Röcken in Prussian Saxony, Nietzsche came from a firmly Protestant background. Both his grandfathers were in clerical positions and his father, Carl Ludwig Nietzsche, was appointed pastor at Röcken by order of King Friedrich Wilhelm IV of Prussia. He died in 1849, and after the death two months later of Nietzsche's younger brother Joseph the stricken family moved to Naumburg on the river Saale. He was brought up in a family consisting entirely of females: his mother Franziska, his younger sister Elisabeth, his maternal grandmother and two maiden aunts. In 1858 he obtained a scholarship to Schulpforta, Germany's leading Protestant boarding school. There he received an outstanding classical education and after his graduation in 1864 he studied theology and classical philology at the University of Bonn.

With this, his final book, he was aiming once and for all to explain, and possibly defend, his work to a world that so far had not taken much notice of his writing. All his adult life he suffered from crippling illnesses that forced him into retirement at the age of only 35. However, this gave him the time he needed to think and to write. Nietzsche saw himself as a missionary and a prophet; he did not write for personal gain or fame. He wanted to confront the world with the truth – his truth: 'I am no man, I am dynamite', he exclaimed.

In *Ecce Homo* he looks back on his literary output and tells us why he wrote these books, where they came from and whether his position had changed at all over the course of the years: overall his answer is 'No' – he stands by his work. He maintained that he 'had the ability to change perspectives' and *re-evaluate his values* – in short that he now knew *how to become who he was* and, moreover, he was against all systems of belief: 'Beware lest a statue crushes you!'

Mental collapse

Unfortunately, much of Nietzsche's work came under the control of others, not least his sister Elisabeth Förster-Nietzsche. She had married a man with strong anti-Semitic leanings and lived with him for many years in South America, far away from her brother's sphere of influence. In 1889, shortly after finishing *Ecce Homo*, Nietzsche suffered a complete mental collapse from which he never recovered. His mother brought him back to Naumburg where she took care of him and, on her death, Elisabeth, who had returned to Germany following her husband's suicide, took him into her home in Weimar, where he died on 25 August 1900.

Nietzsche could no longer look after himself, and gradually she took over the role of curating his work, dismissing previous editors. Thanks to Elisabeth's editorship, the Nazis found it convenient to claim Nietzsche as one of their own. They feasted on the poet-philosopher's polemics and concepts such as the 'Last Man', 'Master-Slave Morality', 'Superman' and the 'Will to Power', all taken out of context and wilfully misunderstood. But Nietzsche's unwavering support for freedom of expression, his attacks on nationalism and his mockery of all forms of anti-Semitism rife in Germany at that time should have made him an enemy of Nazi doctrine. Instead, his writings became so notorious that even today they are sometimes rejected out of hand.

Writer and historian Golo Mann writes in *The History of Germany Since 1789*: 'He [Nietzsche] did not create a system like Kant or Hegel. That was no longer possible for a philosopher around 1880; his imitators may have tried it. Nietzsche's achievement is his life that pulses in his work.' Ironically, Nietzsche, who grew up in the plains of northern Germany, sought refuge in mountains throughout his life. A man far ahead of his time, Nietzsche never followed one line of belief; he jumped from one concept to another – from mountain peak to mountain peak, so to speak. It is pointless to try to pin him down. And this is how we should perhaps read this book: as startling and thought-provoking, but also as an example of poetic intensity and linguistic precision that is almost Goethean in its originality.

Nietzsche began his writing career in a careful and measured way. As a brilliant academic, he was awarded a

PhD in 1869 without a dissertation, as well as being offered a professorship at the University of Basel at the age of only 25. His first book, *The Birth of Tragedy* (1872), was inspired by the works of Richard Wagner and Arthur Schopenhauer, but as we shall see when we read *Ecce Homo*, he came to distance himself from both. In *The Birth of Tragedy* Nietzsche's outstanding contribution to German, and indeed all, literature was the introduction of the struggle between the Dionysian and the Apollonian form – Dionysus is the free, roaming spirit, the god of wine and song; Apollo is theoretical, rigid and restrained. However, both sides exist in all men to a varying degree. This dichotomy inspired the work of Hermann Hesse and Thomas Mann, who were great Nietzsche admirers.

Nietzsche's dictum, 'God is dead', first mentioned in *The Joyful Science* in 1882, remains a battle cry in *Ecce Homo*, but it also set generations of writers and thinkers free to try to find their own meaning of life, without being hampered by the rigid and inflexible rules and strictures of religious institutions.

His book *Human, All Too Human*, written between 1878 and 1880, signifies his middle period in writing and was dedicated to the memory of Voltaire on the hundredth anniversary of his death. In it he adopted the style of 18th-century French writers, blasting his ideas forth in a series of aphorisms, which, if anything, emphasized the revolutionary nature of his message.

'Good European'

He liked to see himself as a freethinker in the true sense of the Enlightenment; his role models were Voltaire, Rousseau and

Stendhal. He called himself a 'good European' and praised Napoleon as an internationalist and possible saviour. Nation states – 'mini states of petty politics', as he calls them – were abhorrent to him. *Ecce Homo* above all is about the concept of 'free will' and 'free spirit'. As he tells us, 'The term "free spirit" cannot have any other meaning here, but that it is *liberated*, a spirit that took control of itself once again.'

The years 1883 to 1887 saw the publications of *Thus Spoke Zarathustra*, in his own eyes his masterpiece, and *Beyond Good and Evil*. By then partially blinded and semi-paralysed, he had to dictate most of the books to his follower, Peter Gast, a young composer who was devoted to him. 'From then on, all my writings are fishhooks: perhaps I am as good an angler as anyone else?… If I caught nothing, it's not my fault. *There just weren't any fish…*', states Nietzsche about his late work.

He also claimed, with some justification, to be a psychologist. When he talks about the instincts and instinctive truths, he is really talking of the subconscious. As such, he is Freud's forerunner; notions which are similar to those of Freud include the concept of the unconscious mind and the idea that repression pushes unacceptable feelings and thoughts into the unconscious so the individual does not have to face up to them.

Giant among thinkers?

So what is it that continues to make Nietzsche an acclaimed giant among the thinkers of the 19th and 20th centuries? Why has the age of modernism not discarded him as a verbose, somewhat boastful writer, seemingly remote from the world, a recluse but not a sage?

Surely the most obvious answer is that he is actually the father of modernism as we know it, as well as an early existentialist. He gave his mouthpiece Zarathustra almost divine status to promote ideas Nietzsche felt he was born to fight for – to release Christians from slavery to the church and ordinary people from the curse of their ordinariness. He wanted to set mankind free. Yet: 'You will look in vain for a trace of fanaticism in my character', he tells us in *Ecce Homo*, and with some pride he recalls a critic who commended his writing 'for its perfect tact in distinguishing between the person and the issue'. He describes his alter-ego Zarathustra as 'the soul which has the longest ladder and can go down the deepest'. How mysterious does 'Superman' become when his creator writes of him: 'Look, how Zarathustra descends and says something kind to everyone! How gently his hands touch even his antagonists, the priests, and how he suffers *with* them.' Even though Nietzsche has created a warrior, he wages war with words not deeds.

Friedrich Nietzsche claims Zarathustra to be the leading philosopher and psychologist of all time, the antichrist, the free spirit, and at times he and his 'Superman' are as one. Is this the boasting of an egocentric recluse, shouting his truth as loud as he can above the din around him? Not so! If we take it that Nietzsche was so tortured by the illiberal times he lived in, that a voice was needed to preach a new message of personal freedom from the mountain peaks, then we make sense of Zarathustra, who, in the end, is a poetic invention conjured into being for just this purpose. But any contradictions should not disturb a postmodern reader who long ago stopped believing in the existence of a safe universe in which there are neat answers to burning questions. Nietzsche does not provide answers; in fact he is re-mining ancient seams of knowledge to ask, to worry and to warn. He foresaw the catastrophes of the 20th century in a way also achieved by Franz Kafka, his fellow prophet.

Above all Nietzsche was an innovative and superb master of the German language. That is why I felt particularly privileged to translate his book, and hope in humility that some echo of his stirring and wonderful words will reach the reader.

In *Ecce Homo*, he harked back to his favourite poet, Heinrich Heine, and claimed that he and Heine had been the 'top jugglers' of the German language. This can be seen in the beauty of Nietzsche's poetry, which is expressed in a curiously pared-down language that crops up here and there like little islands in his otherwise densely knitted prose, nowhere more poignantly than here:

> *They cry the crows*
> *in buzzing flight towards the town*
> *soon it will snow*
> *pity all those without a home*

Gerta Valentine

Translator's note

To make the text more accessible I took the liberty of translating most of the many Latin and French expressions that were strewn throughout the text. A man of letters of the 19th century, Nietzsche would have taken an instant understanding of most of these concepts for granted. Today, even if readers have had a traditional classical education, this way of writing may sometimes seem a little pretentious. Nothing could have been further from what Nietzsche intended.

Another piece of licence within my translation is the use of paragraphs instead of dashes. Dashes are all very well, but while they seem to blend in well enough in the original, they would leave a rather too Germanic feel to the text that may alienate the English reader.

Thus I kept them if a special emphasis was to be made, but in most cases the dashes either denote an ironic wink of the eye, in which case I used brackets, or they had a similar function to paragraphing.

Nietzsche refers to many individuals by name. Some, like Wagner or Schopenhauer, need no explanation, and some are fully explained in the text, but for those that are less well known, I attach a short 'Who's Who' below:

• David Friedrich Strauss (1808–1874) was a German theologian and writer. He impressed scholars with his portrayal of the 'historical Jesus', whose divine nature he denied. Nietzsche criticized Strauss on philosophical grounds.

• Georg Heinrich August Ewald (1803–1875) was a German orientalist and theologian.

• Bruno Bauer (1809–1882) was a German theologian, philosopher and historian who encouraged Nietzsche's criticism of Strauss.

• Friedrich Theodor Vischer (1807–1887) was a German writer on the philosophy of art.

• Dr Heinrich von Stein (1857–1887) was a German philologist, philosopher and dean of the University of Rostock.

• Hans von Bülow (1830–1894) was a contemporary musician and married to Cosima, who later became Wagner's mistress and then wife and mother of three of his children.

• Karl Franz Brendel (1811–1865) was music critic and editor of *Neue Zeitschrift für Musik* and co-editor of *Anregungen für Kunst*.

• Heinrich Gotthard von Treitschke (1834–1896) was a nationalist German historian and political writer during the time of the German Empire who advocated a very aggressive nation state policy.

• Herbert Spencer (1820–1903) was an English philosopher, prominent classical liberal political theorist and sociological theorist of the Victorian era. Spencer developed an all-embracing conception of evolution as the progressive development of the physical world, biological organisms, the human mind, and human culture and societies. He is best known for coining the phrase 'survival of the fittest', which he did in *Principles of Biology* (1864), after reading Charles Darwin's *On the Origin of Species*.

• Peter Gast/Pietro Gasti was Nietzsche's devoted disciple and aide. The nearly-blind philosopher dictated his later work to him and he also acted as proofreader. Nietzsche confessed to admiring his work as a composer very much and they both went to Venice on one occasion. It was Nietzsche's first visit to that city and he was much inspired by it.

There are also numerous place names in *Ecce Homo*. Some are self-evident like Turin, the Upper Engadine and Nice. Schulpforta is mentioned in my introduction; it was a highly acclaimed protestant boarding school in Thuringia, southeast Germany, which Nietzsche attended as a boy. Wörth and Metz are places in Alsace where Nietzsche saw action during the Franco-Prussian war. Rather than referring to the Palazzo de Quirinale, I explained it within the translation as the King of Italy's residence. Tribschen is Wagner's home near the Swiss lake Lucerne, given to him by the Bavarian King Ludwig II. It was here that he and Nietzsche first met.

Nietzsche calls himself a 'philologist by trade' and I kept this description even though modern readers may be puzzled by it. Philology was the precursor to today's linguistics, which has changed to favour spoken data over written data. Comparative linguistics and historical linguistics, in which words from different languages are compared and contrasted to determine the current or historical relationships between languages, have their roots in 19th-century philology. These days, therefore, we would tend to think of a philologist as an expert in linguistics, but that may or may not include literature, which of course is Nietzsche's greatest contribution to intellectual life and the German language. 'Philology' literally means 'love of words', and the field often deals with literature more than other branches of linguistics do. In the modern academic world, philology is usually understood to mean the study of written texts, usually ancient ones. It was much more common in the 19th century than it is today for a linguist to be called a philologist.

On pages 44–5, Nietzsche refers to the year 1866 as being significant for him. It was in that year he started to depart from philology and turned towards philosophy.

The 'Junker' philosophy is a specifically German concept; it refers in general to the land-owning classes.

Nietzsche referred to his 'Four Untimely Meditations' as 'The Untimely Ones', but for greater clarity, this translation refers to them as meditations. By 'untimely' he really means avant garde.

The most difficult problems posed to a translator are where figures of speech or puns are deeply entwined either within the German language or Nietzsche's time or culture, or when they were new inventions of Nietzsche's own ingenious mind or even any combination of these. Here I have tried to repair the holes that they may have left in the text.

In section one of 'The Wagner Case', he writes about the founding of a 'Liszt society' to sponsor and spread '*listige Kirchenmusik*' (literally: cunning church music), making fun of the composer's name. To keep the pun, I used 'listed' church music as in registered and officially recognized church music which would be an attack on German bureaucracy.

In section three of the same chapter he writes about German philosophers Fichte, Schelling, Schopenhauer, Hegel, Schleiermacher, Kant and Leibniz and adds that they are all 'Schleiermacher' (literally veil makers), again making fun of a name. What he means is that they are all only pulling the wool over our eyes, which I used. The literal translation would have been wooden and meaningless to English eyes.

In section four of this chapter (probably the most idiosyncratic chapter of the whole book) Nietzsche refers to a 'savouress of Capitoline Hill'; he is, I believe, referring to a goose or to geese belonging to an area on Capitoline Hill in Rome, dedicated to the goddess Juno; their gabbling woke up a group of Roman soldiers just in time to defend the hill against an attack by the Gauls. I translated it as 'some silly goose' because the comment would otherwise not have been understood – indeed, it puzzled many contemporary critics and reviewers of Nietzsche. Forgive the misogynistic insinuation, but Nietzsche was at times harsh about women even though some of his aphorisms could be included in a feminist textbook; as I said in my introduction, his views are never too consistent.

Gerta Valentine

Preface

SINCE, SOONER OR LATER, I shall have to approach mankind with one of the most difficult tasks that has ever been asked of it, it seems inevitable that I must tell you *who I am*. It should really be known already: after all, I did present plenty of 'evidence'. However, the disproportion between the greatness of my task and the *triviality* of my peers has manifested itself in that I have not been heard, nor even been seen. I live on my own credit; is it perhaps just a preconception that I actually live?... I only need to speak to one of those 'learned men' that come visiting the Upper Engadine during the summer to become convinced that I do not live... Under such circumstances there is a duty against which my way of life, and quintessentially even more so my instincts revolt, that is to say: *Listen to me! for I am who I am. Above all, do not take me for someone else!*

2.

FOR INSTANCE, I am by no means a bogey man, nor am I a moral monster – far from it, I am actually the opposite to the type of man that hitherto has been admired as virtuous. Between you and me, I am really quite proud of it. I am a follower of the philosopher Dionysus; I should prefer to be a satyr rather than a saint. Just read this book to see what I mean. Perhaps I was able to throw some light on this polarity in a happy and philanthropic way, perhaps this was the only point of this book. The last thing *I* should promise is to try and 'improve' mankind. You will not find me erecting new idols! The old may come to realize what it means to have feet of clay! To *topple* Idols (my word for 'ideals') comes somewhat closer to my craft. They deprived reality of its worth, its meaning, its truthfulness to the same extent to which they have *fabricated* an ideal world... The 'true world' and the 'apparent world', or to say it more plainly: th*e fabricated* world and reality... The *lie* of the ideal has until now been the curse on reality; mankind itself has on account of it become dishonest and false down to its basest instincts – to the point of worshipping the *opposite* values from those which alone would guarantee success, a future, the lofty *right* to a future.

3.

THOSE WHO can breathe the air of my writing know that it is the air at the top of the mountains, a *strong* air. You have to be made for it, otherwise there is no small danger of catching cold from it. Ice is all around you, the loneliness is immense – but how quietly all things lie in the light! How freely you breathe! How much you feel lies *beneath* you! – Philosophy, as I have so far understood and lived it, is the voluntary life among ice and high mountains – seeking all that is foreign and dubious in existence, all that which so far has been outlawed by morality. From long experience, acquired on such a journey through *the forbidden*, I learned to look at the causes, which until now prompted moralizing and idealizing, in a very different light than may have been desired: the *hidden* history of the philosophers, the psychology of their great names became clear to me.

How much truth can the mind *bear*, how much truth does it *dare* to take in? This became more and more my real yardstick. Error (– faith in the ideal –) is not blindness, error is *cowardice*... Every accomplishment, every step forward in knowledge is a *consequence* of courage, from being hard on yourself, from your own cleanliness... I do not refute ideals, I merely put on gloves when I deal with them... We strive for the *forbidden*: under this sign, my philosophy shall triumph one day for they have basically always forbidden the truth alone.

4.

MY *ZARATHUSTRA* is unique among my books. With it, I gave mankind the most precious gift that it has been given up to now. This book, its voice spanning thousands of years, is not only the loftiest book in existence, a true mountain air book – the whole fact of what man is lies incredibly far *beneath* him – it is actually also the *deepest*, born out of the innermost wealth of truth, an inexhaustible well, where no pail will descend without coming up again brimming with gold and goodness. Here speaks no 'prophet', none of those dreadful hybrids of sickness and will to power commonly known as religious founders. Above all, you have to *hear* the tone coming from that mouth, this peaceful tone, as it should be *heard*, so you do not misjudge the sense of its wisdom in some wretched way.

'It is the stillest words which bring about the storm; thoughts that creep up on you with the footsteps of doves steer the world.

The figs are falling from the trees, they are good and sweet; and as they fall, their red skin bursts.

I am a north wind to ripe figs.

Thus, like figs, these teachings fall into your laps, my friends; now you drink their juice and their sweet meat.

Autumn is around us and pure sky and afternoon.'

It is no fanatic that speaks here, this is not 'preaching', there is no *faith* required here: drop by drop, word upon word falls from an immeasurable abundance of light and depth of happiness – their timing is a tender slow movement. Such things will only reach the chosen few; it is a privilege without equal to be a listener here; nobody should expect as a matter of course to have an ear for Zarathustra… In view of all that, is Zarathustra not a *seducer* after all?… But what does he himself say as he returns for the first time to his solitude? Precisely the opposite of everything that any old 'sage', 'saint', 'world-redeemer' or other Decadent would say in such a case… Not only does he talk differently, he actually *is* different…

'I shall now go away to be alone, my disciples. You too will go now and be alone. That is how I wish it.

Depart from me and defend yourself against Zarathustra. And better still: be ashamed of him! Perhaps he has deceived you. Man of knowledge must not just love his enemies, he must also be able to hate his friends.

You reward your teacher poorly if you always remain a pupil. And why do you not wish to pluck at my laurels?

You venerate me: but what if your veneration should one day *collapse*? Beware lest a statue crushes you!

You say, you believe in Zarathustra? But why does Zarathustra matter!

You are my believers, but why do believers matter!

You had not even looked for each other: yet you found me.

That is the way with all believers; that is why all beliefs matter so little.

Now I bid you to lose me and to find yourselves and only *when you have all denied me* shall I come back to you.'

FRIEDRICH NIETZSCHE

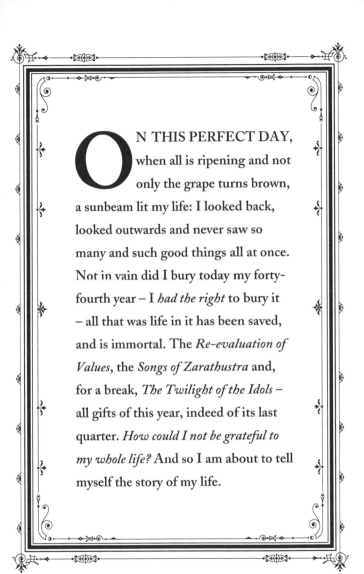

ON THIS PERFECT DAY, when all is ripening and not only the grape turns brown, a sunbeam lit my life: I looked back, looked outwards and never saw so many and such good things all at once. Not in vain did I bury today my forty-fourth year – I *had the right* to bury it – all that was life in it has been saved, and is immortal. The *Re-evaluation of Values*, the *Songs of Zarathustra* and, for a break, *The Twilight of the Idols* – all gifts of this year, indeed of its last quarter. *How could I not be grateful to my whole life?* And so I am about to tell myself the story of my life.

Chapter 1

Why I am so wise

1.

THE HAPPINESS of my existence, its uniqueness perhaps, lies in its inevitable end: I am, to put it in the form of a riddle, as my own father, already dead; as my own mother, I am still alive and grow old. This duality, taken as it were from the highest and lowest rungs of the ladder of life, at once decadent and a *beginning* – this, if anything, explains that neutrality, that freedom from involvement in the general problems of life, which are perhaps so typical for me. I have always had a keener nose for early indications of the rise and downfall than any other person; in this I am the perfect teacher – I know both, I am both.

My father died at thirty-six: he was delicate, lovable, and morbid, as any being that is only meant to live for a brief spell – a gentle reminder of life rather than life itself. During the same year in which his life declined, mine too declined: in my thirty-sixth year I reached the lowest point of my vitality – I was still alive but could not see three steps ahead of me. At that time – it was in 1879 – I resigned my professorship in Basel, lived throughout the summer like a shadow in St Moritz and the following winter, the most sun-starved of my life, *as* a shadow in Naumburg. This was the lowest point of my existence; *The Wanderer and his Shadow* was the product of this period. No doubt, I was an expert in shadows then…

The following winter, my first winter in Genoa, brought forth that sweetness and spirituality which almost always goes hand in hand with an extreme physical weakness: my book *Dawn*. The perfect brightness and cheerfulness, even exuberance of the spirit that this work reflects, is not, in my case, just consistent with the most profound physiological weakness, but also with an excess of suffering. In the midst of the agony caused by three days of headaches accompanied by violent attacks of nausea with hopeless retching of bile – I was possessed of extraordinary dialectical clarity and in utter cold blood I thought things through, which in a healthier frame of mind I would not have been smart enough, not *cold* enough a mountaineer to do. My readers may know how far I regard dialectic as a symptom of decadence, for instance in the most notorious case of all: the case of Socrates.

All the morbid disturbances of the intellect, even that semi-stupor which follows a fever, have remained alien to me to this very day, and I had to inform myself first on their nature and frequency, looking it up in books. My blood runs slowly through my veins. No-one has ever seen me run a temperature. A doctor who treated me over a longer period as a neurotic patient finally decided: 'No, there is nothing the matter with your nerves; quite simply, I am the one who is nervous.' There is absolutely no sign of any local degeneration; no stomach upset caused by organ failure, despite the profound weakness of the gastric systems which comes from my general exhaustion. Even my eye trouble, sometimes coming dangerously close to blindness, is just an effect, not a cause, so that as my physical strength increased, my visual power also increased.

A long, much too long, number of years means recovery for me, unfortunately though, it also means relapse, decline, a spell of decadence. After all this, need I say that I am *experienced* in matters of decadence? I know it backwards! Even that finely spun craft of apprehension and comprehension in general, that feeling for nuances, that psychology of 'seeing what is around the corner' and whatever else I may be able to do, was first learned at that point, and it is the very gift of that period during which everything in me became refined, observation itself as well as the organs of observation. To look upon *healthier* concepts and values from the standpoint of the sick man and, conversely, to look down from the abundance and self-confidence of a *rich* life down into the secret workings of the instinct of decadence – that has been my main task, the one I worked longest at, in which if anything at all, I became expert. I have it at my fingertips now, I have the ability to *change perspectives*, the main reason perhaps, why I alone could achieve a *Re-evaluation of Values*.

2.

IF YOU ACCEPT that I am decadent, I am also the opposite. My argument for this amongst other things is that I always instinctively choose the *proper* means to fight bad conditions: whilst the Decadent, as such, invariably chooses those means that are to his disadvantage. Overall, then, I was of sound health, but looked at more closely, I was decadent.

That energy for absolute isolation and extraction from a life of habit, the way I forced myself no longer to be indulged, to be waited on hand and foot, to be *pampered* – all that proves the absolute certainty of my instincts *that was*, above all, essential for me at that time. I took myself in hand, I healed myself: this can only be done on the condition – as every physician will admit – that we are *basically healthy*. A typically morbid being cannot become healthy at all, much less heal himself: whereas for a typically healthy being illness can even be a strong *stimulus* to life, for an even richer life. This, indeed, is how I *now* regard my long period of illness: I discovered life afresh, as it were, myself included; I tasted all good and even trifling things in such a way that others cannot easily do – I created my philosophy from my will for health, for *life*…

For I must ask you to take note of this; it was during those years when my life-force was at its lowest ebb that I *ceased* being a pessimist: the instinct of self-recovery forbade me to adopt a philosophy of poverty and discouragement… Now, how can we basically recognize *brilliance*? We recognize that a brilliant or first-rate human being is agreeable to our senses: that he is made of a matter at once hard yet sweet and fragrant. He enjoys only what is conducive to him; his pleasure, his desire ceases as soon as the level of what is good for him has been overstepped. He divines remedies against injuries, he uses serious accidents to his own advantage; that which does not kill him makes him stronger. He instinctively gathers his *sum-total* from all that he sees, hears and experiences. He is a selective principle, he discards much. He is always in *his own* company, whether he deals with books, people or landscapes:

he honours his *choices* by *acknowledging* them, by *trusting* them. He reacts slowly to all types of stimuli, with the very slowness bred in him by long years of caution and deliberate pride – he tests the stimulus that meets him head-on; no compromise is required. He believes in neither 'misfortune' nor 'guilt'; he copes with himself and others; he knows *when to let go* – he is strong enough to turn everything to his greatest advantage.

Well then, I am the opposite of a Decadent: for I just described none other than *myself*.

3.

I REGARD it as a great privilege to have had such a father; the peasants he preached to (for, after having lived for some years at the Altenburg Court, he spent his last years of life as a preacher) said of him that this is how the angels must have looked – and with this I will touch on the question of race.

I am a Polish nobleman without a drop of bad blood, least of all German blood. If I search for the most shocking contrast to myself, the unfathomable pettiness of the instincts, I always find my mother and sister – to believe myself kindred to such bitches would be blaspheming my divinity. The treatment that I have received from my mother and sister fills me with unutterable horror to this very day; there is a totally hellish machine at work here, operating with infallible certainty at the precise moment when I am most vulnerable – at my loftiest moments. For then I lack any strength to defend myself against such vipers! The physiological closeness makes such age-old disharmony possible – but I confess that the deepest objection against any 'reincarnation' and my real thoughts when staring into the abyss, are always of my mother and sister.

However, even as a Pole I am an incredible throwback. You would have to go back centuries to find this noblest race that ever lived on earth as sensitive as I have described them. Everything that is called noble these days gives me a feeling of superiority and distinction – I would not allow the young German Emperor the honour of being my coachman. There is one single case where I acknowledge my equal and I admit it with profound gratitude: Madame Cosima Wagner is by far the noblest nature; and, I may as well admit it, I hold true that Richard Wagner was the man by far closest akin to me; the rest – silence!

All prevailing concepts about degrees of relationship are an utter physiological nonsense. Even today the Pope insists on this absurdity for his own purposes. We are least akin to our parents; indeed it would be the utmost mark of vulgarity to be too akin to our parents. Loftier natures can trace their true origins infinitely farther back; from them a great deal had to be gathered, hoarded and heaped over long periods of time. The great individuals are the oldest; I do not understand why, but Julius Caesar could have been my father – or Alexander, that Dionysus incarnate… At the very moment of writing this, someone has sent me the head of Dionysus through the mail…

4.

I NEVER understood the art of being antagonistic – this, too, I owe to my marvellous father – even though at times it could have been very useful to me. However unchristian this may seem, I do not even feel antagonism against myself. You can look at my life from any angle and rarely will you find traces of any ill will towards me (apart from that one single case perhaps), though too many traces of *good will*...

Even my experiences with those that everyone else fares badly with are without exception positive; I tame every beast, I can even make buffoons behave demurely. During the seven years in which I taught classical Greek to a top form at the Grammar school in Basel, I never needed to administer a punishment. Even the laziest worked hard for me in my class. If chance comes my way, I will take it, but I have to be spontaneous to take control of myself. Whatever the instrument, however badly tuned, even if as much out of tune as only the instrument 'man' can be – I would have to be ill if I could not squeeze something worth listening to out of it. And as often as not, I have been told by the 'instruments' themselves that they had thought themselves incapable of such a tune...

Most beautifully perhaps by that Heinrich von Stein who died unforgivably young, and who, after dutifully obtaining permission, turned up and stayed for three days in Sils-Maria, explaining to everyone that he had *not* just come to look at the Engadine. This fine human being, who waded deep into Wagnerian mires (and also into those of Dürer!) with all the impetuous simplicity of a Prussian nobleman, became a different man during these three days, changed by a tempest of freedom like one who has been suddenly lifted to *his* full height and given wings to fly with. I told him over and again that it was the good mountain air up here that did it, that everyone felt like that, that after all, you were not some 6,000 ft above Bayreuth for nothing – but he would not believe me…

If, in spite of that, some small and not so small misdemeanours have been committed against me, it was not an act of 'will', least of all of *ill* will: rather, as I have already indicated, I could complain of good will that has done no little mischief in my life. My experiences give me a right to feel generally suspicious of the so-called 'selfless' instincts, the whole concept of 'neighbourly love', that is always ready to offer advice or to break into action. I deem it a weakness in itself, an individual case of inability to resist temptations – only the Decadent call *compassion* a virtue. I accuse the compassionate of easily losing modesty, respect, the sensitivity to keep their distance; compassion smells very quickly of the mob and is indistinguishable from bad manners – compassionate hands can at times be interfering in a downright destructive way with a great destiny, the growing isolation amongst the wounded and the *privilege* of a great wrong. I count conquering compassion among the *noble* virtues: with the 'Temptation of Zarathustra' I wrote a poem where a great cry of distress reaches his ear, where compassion assaults him and tries to entice him away from *himself* like a final sin. To keep control of himself at this point, to remain adamant that the *magnitude* of his task must not be belittled by lower and more short-sighted impulses which affect the so-called selfless deeds, that is the test, perhaps the ultimate test, which Zarathustra must pass – the real *proof* of power.

5.

AND IN YET another respect I am once more my father over again and thus the continuation of his life following his so untimely death. Like every man who has never lived amongst equals and to whom therefore the notion of 'retaliation' is just as foreign as the notion of 'equal rights', I do not allow myself to safeguard or protect myself when small or even gross acts of foolishness have been committed against me – naturally, neither do I defend or justify myself. My kind of retaliation is quickly to send prudence to run after stupidity, perhaps it will catch up with it. To put it as a parable: I eat a pot of jam in order to get rid of a *sour* taste... Just let anyone speak ill of me, I shall 'retaliate', don't doubt it: it won't take me long to find an opportunity to offer my thanks to the 'perpetrator' (occasionally even for the misdeed itself) – or to *ask* him for something, which can be more gracious even than *offering* something...

Moreover, it seems to me that the rudest word, the rudest letter, is still kinder, still more virtuous than silence. Those who are silent are almost always lacking in delicacy and refinement of the heart; silence is an objection, swallowing grievances makes for a bad character – it even upsets the stomach. All those who are silent suffer from dyspepsia.

As you see, I do not wish to underestimate rudeness, it is by far the most *human* form of contradiction and amidst the modern fashion for pampering, one of our most important virtues.

If you are rich enough for it, it may even be your good fortune to be in the wrong. A god descending to this earth could *do* nothing but wrong; not to bring punishment on himself but to take on the *guilt* – only that would make him divine.

6.

TO BE FREE of resentment, to be aware of resentment – who knows how much I ultimately have to thank my long illness for, even for that. The problem is not an easy one: you have to have experienced it from strength as well as from weakness. If anything has to be upheld against illness, against weakness, it is that man's actual sense of salvation, that is to say his *instinct for war and taking up arms* has been worn out. We know how to break free from nothingness, we know how to cope with nothingness, we know how to push nothingness away from us – it all hurts. Man and things crowd in, all experiences strike too deep, memory is a festering wound. Illness itself is a form of resentment.

In the face of that, the sick man has only one great remedy – I call it *Russian fatalism*, that fatalism without revolt with which a Russian soldier lies down in the snow at the end of a campaign that was all too hard; to accept nothing further, to take nothing on, nothing in – to cease reacting altogether...

The great sense in such fatalism (that is not always merely the courage to die, for it can be life-saving under deadly circumstances) lies in reducing the metabolism, slowing it down as a form of will to hibernate. If we take this reasoning a few steps further, we arrive at the fakir who sleeps for weeks in a tomb. Because we would wear ourselves out much too quickly *if* we reacted in any way, we don't react at all: that is the principle. And nothing burns us up faster than the emotion of resentment. Anger, morbid sensitivity, the inability to force revenge, the yearning, the thirst for revenge, the concoction of all types of poison – this, surely, is for the exhausted the most detrimental way to react: it involves a rapid consumption of nervous energy, a pathological increase of harmful secretions, for instance that of bile into the stomach. Resentment is *all that is* forbidden to the sick man – it is his *worst evil*: unfortunately, it is also what he most desires.

That was recognized by that profound physician Buddha. His 'religion' which should rather be called a *hygiene system* to avoid any confusion with such a wretched thing as Christianity, works because it depends on the conquest of resentment: to free the soul of it – this is the first step towards recovery. 'Animosity is not ended by animosity, animosity is ended by friendship'; thus begins Buddha's doctrine – this is *not* the voice of morality but of physiology. Resentment born of weakness is harmful to no-one more than to the weak man himself – conversely, with a fundamentally rich nature it is a *superfluous* emotion, which, if kept under control, is almost a proof of riches. Those readers who know how seriously my philosophy has taken up the fight against the feelings of revenge and rancour, even taking on the doctrine of 'free will' (the fight against Christianity is merely a small part of it), will understand why I emphasise my own personal attitude, my *instinctive confidence* in practicality at precisely this point.

During my decadent period I *denied* myself these feelings as being harmful; as soon as life offered once again wealth and pride, I denied them myself as being beneath me. That 'Russian fatalism' of which I spoke manifested itself in such a way that for years I clung tenaciously to almost unbearable conditions, locations, dwellings, societies, once fate had sent them my way; it was better than changing them, better than *feeling* they could be changed – better than rebelling against them…

Anyone who interfered with my fatalism, who tried forcefully to awaken me, would have been my mortal enemy in those days; in truth, it would have been fatally dangerous every time. Thinking of yourself as a destiny, not wanting to be 'other' than you are – that is under such circumstances the *highest wisdom.*

7.

NOW, WAR IS a different matter altogether. I am essentially a warrior. To wage war is one of my instincts. Talent for animosity, to actually *be* an enemy – this, perhaps, presupposes a strong nature; in any case it is a precondition of every strong nature. It needs resistances, therefore it *seeks* out resistance: *aggressiv*e pathos is just as necessary for strength as resentment and rancour for weakness. Women, for instance, are vengeful: that is due to their weakness, as much as to their sensitivity to others' distress.

The strength of the aggressor, in a way, has its *measure* in the opposition he requires; any increase in strength makes itself known when seeking out a mightier opponent or, indeed, problem – for a philosopher who is a warrior will also do battle with problems. The task is *not* to overcome opponents at all costs, but only those against whom you must pit all your strength, subtlety and fighting skill – opponents who are *your equals*... Equality before the enemy – that is the main condition to fight a *fair* duel. Where you have contempt, you *cannot* wage war; where you are in command, where you can see someone *beneath* you, you *should not* wage war. My war tactics can be summed up in four theorems. Firstly: I only ever engage with causes that are winnable – if necessary, I wait until they win. Secondly: I only ever engage with causes where I would find no allies, where I stand alone – where I compromise only myself... I have never publicly taken a single step which did not compromise me: that is my criterion for doing right. Thirdly: I never attack people – I use a person merely as a powerful magnifying glass that allows me to make visible a general but insidious and elusive calamity.

In this way I attacked David Strauss, or to put it more plainly, the *success* of a senile book amongst the 'cultured classes' of Germany – thereby catching this culture red-handed...

In this way I attacked Wagner, or to put it more plainly, the hypocrisy, the semi-refined instinct of our 'culture' which confuses the artful with richness, the late with the great. Fourthly: I only ever attack things from which all personal differences are excluded, where any background of bad experience is lacking. On the contrary, to attack is to me a proof of good-will, in some circumstances even of gratitude.

It is an honour, a reward, if I associate my name with a matter or a person, notwithstanding whether I am for it or against it. If I wage war on Christianity I have a right to do so, because it's not going to kill me and they're not going to stop me – the most serious Christians were always favourably disposed towards me. I myself, the strictest opponent of Christianity, am far from minded to bear grudges against individuals for what has been the undoing of centuries.

8.

MAY I POINT OUT to you one more trait of my character, which causes me no little difficulty in my dealings with men? I have a perfectly uncanny sense of purity so that I can register, even *smell* the approach or – may I say? – the innermost region, the 'entrails' of every soul in a physical way... This sensitivity of mine has psychological antennae with which I probe and handle every secret: the *hidden* filth at the bottom of many a character. Perhaps caused by bad genes but glossed over by breeding, it is nevertheless obvious to me almost at a glance. If I am right, those who offend my sense of purity also sense my disgust themselves; that does not make them smell any better... To be treated with extreme fairness is a precondition for my existence; I should perish in impure conditions (I got used to swimming and bathing and splashing, as it were, incessantly in water, in some perfectly transparent and glistening element). That is why dealing with men is no small test of my patience; my humanity *does not* consist of empathizing with men's nature but to *endure* that I empathize – my humanity is a constant test of my willpower...

However, I do need *seclusion*, that is to say, healing, being myself again, breathing free, light, playful air… All of my *Zarathustra* is a song in praise of seclusion, or, if you get my meaning, of *purity* – fortunately not about *pure folly*. Those with an eye for colour would call him adamantine; the *loathing* for mankind, for the 'rabble' was always my greatest danger… Do you wish to hear what Zarathustra has to say when he talks of being *set free* of *loathing*?

'What could have happened to me? How have I freed myself from loathing? Who renewed my sight? How did I soar to such heights, above the rabble sitting by the well?

Was it my loathing that gave me wings and water-divining powers?

Truly, I had to fly to the loftiest heights to find once again that fount of desire!

Ah, but I found it, my brothers! Here in the loftiest height the fount of my desire wells up for me, and there is a life in which the rabble cannot have a share.

You flow almost too fast for me, my fount of desire! And often you empty the cup again by wanting to refill it.

And yet I must learn to approach you with greater modesty – my heart overflows all too wildly at the sight of you – my heart, on which my summer's heat is burning; the short, hot, sad, overly blissful one – how my summer heart longs for your chill.

Gone is the lingering sadness of my spring! Gone are the snowflakes of my wickedness in June! I have become all summer and a summer's noon.

A summer in loftiest heights with ice-cold springs and

blissful silence: come, my friends, come that this silence may be still more blissful.

For this is *our* height and our home – we all live here, where it is too high and steep for any of the impure and their thirst. Look with your pure eyes into the fount of my desire, friends! Why should that cloud it? Why, it will smile at you in its *own* purity.

On the tree of future we shall build our nest; eagles will carry food to us recluses in their beaks.

Truly, this is no food that the impure are allowed to share! Like fire it would burn their mouths.

Truly, we do not prepare homes for the impure! Our happiness would be like icy caves to their bodies and spirits.

And like strong winds we shall live above them, neighbours to the eagles, neighbours of the snow, neighbours of the sun: this is the way strong winds live.

And like a wind I shall yet blow amongst them one day and take their spirits' breath away with mine: that is the dictate of my future.

Truly, Zarathustra is a strong wind on all and every plain, and his advice to all his friends and all that spit and spout is this: beware of spitting *against* the wind!…'

Chapter 2
Why I am so clever

1.

WHY DO I KNOW *more* than other people? Why, in general, am I so clever? I have never wasted my time pondering questions that are not really questions. For instance, I have no personal experiences of real *religious* difficulties. It completely escapes me why I should be a 'sinner'. Similarly, I don't have a reliable criterion by which to work out what a bad conscience consists of: from where I stand, a bad conscience does not appear of great value to me... I would rather not leave anything that I have done *afterwards* in the lurch; I would prefer to omit a bad ending, or its *consequences*, from any form of evaluation. A bad ending makes you lose the vision you had in sight, a bad conscience is in my view some form of *evil eye*. To respect something that didn't work all the more because it didn't work – that is rather closer to my set of morals.

'God', 'immortality of the soul', 'redemption', 'heaven', these are all terms for which I never had any time and to which I never paid any attention, even as a child – was I perhaps not enough of a child for that?

For me, atheism is not at all a result, even less an event: to me it is instinctive. I am much too inquisitive, too sceptical, and too high-spirited to put up with an obvious if coarse answer. God is such a coarse and obvious answer, a lack of delicacy towards us thinkers – at heart He is just a coarse command not to think: thou shalt not think!

Now, the question of nutrition is a very different matter to me; on that the 'salvation of mankind' is truly dependent, much more so than on some theological musing. For practical purposes we could put it like this: 'How precisely must you feed yourself to attain your maximum power, a truly enlightened virtue, a virtue free of moral input?'

Here, my personal experiences are the worst possible; I am surprised that I did not become aware of this question earlier, that I have learned to 'reason' from these experiences only at such a late stage. The utter worthlessness of our German culture alone – its 'idealism' – can explain to some extent why of all people I was so backward here, almost revelling in this backwater. This 'culture', which teaches you from the start to lose sight of *reality*, so that you may aim for quite difficult, so-called 'ideal' goals; for instance 'classical education' (as if it was not already doomed to unite the two concepts: 'Classical' and 'German'). Actually, this is quite funny: imagine a man from Leipzig with a classical education!

As it is, in moral terms I have eaten *a very poor diet* until very recently: that is 'impersonally', 'selflessly', 'altruistically' – for the good of the cooks and other fellow Christians. For instance, because of the cuisine of Leipzig as well as my first involvement with the works of Schopenhauer (1865), I seriously shunned my 'will to live'. Think – to upset my stomach on account of a poor diet – such a problem seemed to be amazingly well solved by this type of cuisine (it is said that the year 1866 had brought about a change in this department).

But as to German cuisine in general – what can it not be accused of! Serving soup *before* the main meal (still called *alla tedesca* in 16th-century Venetian cookery books); meat boiled to death, vegetables full of grease and made stodgy with flour; the degeneration of pastries into solid bulk! Add to this the almost bestial, postprandial habits of the ancient, although not just the *ancient* Germans, you will understand the origin of the *German* mind – it is founded in disordered innards. The German mind is a sore stomach; it cannot take any more.

But even the *English* diet that, compared with the German or the French one, seems to me a 'return to nature' (that is, to cannibalism), is deeply repugnant to my innermost self; I think it makes the mind heavy-footed, gives it the feet of English women… My favourite cuisine is that of *Piedmont.*

Alcohol does not agree with me; a glass of wine or beer a day is enough to turn my life into a valley of tears – my adversaries live in Munich. I confess that I came to understand all this a little late, even though I have *experienced* it since childhood. As a boy I believed that drinking wine, like smoking tobacco, was simply youthful vanity, which would then turn into a bad habit. Perhaps the wine of Naumburg vineyards was partly responsible for my harsh judgment. To believe that wine is *cheering* I would have to be a Christian, in other words I would have to believe in what to me is utterly absurd.

Oddly enough, whereas *small* doses of alcohol depress me deeply, *large* quantities turn me almost into a sailor on leave. Even as a boy I could hold my own in this respect. To compose and even transcribe a long Latin essay in a single night, keen to emulate my role model Sallust in austerity and terseness and then to pour some strong drink all over it, this was not incompatible with my physiology even as a pupil of the venerable grammar school Schulpforta, perhaps not even to that of Sallust – however much it was frowned upon by that venerable school… But later in life I decided against any form of 'spirit' as a drink; like Richard Wagner who converted me, I, an opponent of vegetarianism from experience, cannot urge all those with a *fine* mind strongly enough to entirely abstain from alcohol. Water is good enough… I prefer locations where I have an opportunity to drink water fresh from a fountain, for instance in Nice, Turin and Sils; I keep a small glass by me wherever I go.

In wine lies the truth – here too I seem to be at odds with the rest of the world about the concept of 'truth' – for me, the spirit floats above *water*. Let me give you a few more pieces of advice from my set of moral codes. A big meal is easier to digest than a small one. A main condition for a good digestive system is the fact that the stomach has to work in its entirety. You ought *to know* the size of your stomach. For the same reasons I advise against those lengthy meals, which I call interrupted sacrificial feasts and which are served at the *table d'hôte*.

No snacking in between, no coffee, coffee is depressing. Tea is only good in the morning, in small quantities but strong. If too weak, even by a grain or two, tea can be very harmful and leave you indisposed for the whole day. Everyone has their own limits, sometimes within the narrowest and most delicate margins. In a very irritating climate I advise against drinking tea first thing in the morning. If at all possible, drink a cup of strong cocoa, any cocoa butter extracted, an hour beforehand. *Sit* on your bottom as little as possible; trust no thought that is not born in the open and in free motion, when all your muscles are engaged. All prejudices come from the bowels. The bottom – I said it before – is the true *sin* against the Holy Spirit.

2.

THE QUESTION of nutrition is closely related to that of *location* and *climate*. None of us can live everywhere at the same time, and those of us who have to perform great tasks which require all our strength have an even more limited choice. The influence of climate upon the *metabolism*, slowing it down or speeding it up, is so great that a wrong choice of location and climate not only alienates you from your task but can even prevent you from taking it up altogether: you would never even know it. Thus, animal strength has never been developed enough to feel that exuberant freedom which enables you to recognize: Only I can do *that*.

Even the least sluggishness of the bowels, once a habit, is more than enough to turn the genius into something mediocre, something 'German'. The climate of Germany alone is sufficient to discourage the strongest and most heroic bowels. The timing of the metabolism is in precise relation to the agility or slowness of the mind's *feet*: after all, the 'mind' itself is only a form of this metabolism. Put together locations where ingenious people live and always have lived, where wit, cleverness, and irony were part of happiness, where genius is almost compelled to dwell: all of these places have an exquisitely dry atmosphere. Paris, Provence, Florence, Jerusalem, Athens (these names prove something: Genius is *dependent* on dry air, on clear skies), in other words, on a rapid metabolism, on being able to continuously supply itself with great, even enormous quantities of power. I have a case in mind where a great and open mind became narrow, repressed, pedantic and cranky, simply because it lacked a fine instinct for climate. I myself might have become such a case, if illness had not forced me to reason and to reflect upon reason realistically. Now long practice has taught me to read the effects of climatic and meteorological origin on myself as on a very precise and reliable instrument, so that after a journey even as short as that from Turin to Milan I can calculate the change in the degree of atmospheric humidity by observing my body, and I remember with horror the *sinister* fact that apart from the last ten years, the most dangerous years, my life was always spent at the wrong locations, places that should have been forbidden to me: Naumburg, Schulpforta, Thuringia in general, Leipzig, Basel – so many disastrous places for my constitution. If I have not a single pleasant memory of my childhood and youth it would be foolish to blame it at this point on so-called 'moral' causes, as for instance the incontestable lack of *compatible* company; for this lack exists today just as it did then and it does not stop me from being cheerful and brave. But it was the ignorance of the functioning of the body, that confounded 'idealism', that was the real curse of my life, superfluous and stupid, from which no good would come, for which there can be no compensation, no agreement. The consequences of this 'idealism' explain all my blunders, the great aberrations of instinct and the 'modesties' that diverted me from my task, the fact that I became a professor of linguistics – why not at least a medical doctor or anything else that could have opened my eyes? During my stay in Basel, my whole intellectual routine, including my daily schedule, was a completely pointless abuse of extraordinary powers, without any sort of compensation for the strength I had spent, without even giving a thought about its exhaustion and how to replace it. I completely lacked any subtle egotism; I did not take care of my imperious instinct; I was everyone's equal – it was a 'selflessness' that did not observe distance – something I will never forgive myself for. When I had almost reached the end (*because* I very nearly did reach it), I began to reflect on this basic absurdity of my life, which was 'idealism'. It was my *illness* that brought me to reason.

3.

CHOICE OF nutrition, choice of climate and location: the third choice, where you must not at any price go wrong, is *your* choice of *recreation*. Here again, depending on the uniqueness of your mind, the limits of what is permitted (that is to say *useful*) are ever more restricted. In my case, general *reading* is part of my recreation, therefore it is part of that which allows me to escape from myself, that lets me stroll through alien sciences and souls – something I no longer take seriously.

Indeed, reading allows me to recover from my seriousness. When I work very intensely, you do not find books near me: I wouldn't dream of letting anyone talk to me or even think in my presence. After all, that is just what reading means…

Has anyone ever noticed that, that during that profound tension to which the state of pregnancy condemns the mind and basically the entire organism, chance and every kind of external stimulus strike much too vehemently and 'penetrate' too deeply? You must try to avoid accidents and external stimuli as far as possible: to brick yourself in is one of the first instinctive precautions of spiritual pregnancy. Would I permit an *alien* thought to secretly climb over my brick wall? – After all, that is just what reading means…

Periods of work and productivity are followed by a period of recreation: come on, you pleasant, you witty, you clever books! – Will they be German books?

I must go back six months to catch myself with a book in my hand. What was it this time? An excellent work by Victor Brochard, *Les Sceptiques Grecs*. The sceptics, the only *venerable* types amongst the two-faced, indeed quintuple-faced race of philosophers!

Otherwise, I almost always take refuge in the same books, not very many really, such books that seem to have been written for me. Perhaps it is not in my nature to read many or a wide variety of books: a library makes me ill. Neither is it in my nature to love many or, indeed, a wide variety of things. Suspicion, even hostility towards new books, is more likely to be one of my instincts than 'tolerance', 'generosity' and other types of 'brotherly love'. Ultimately, it is to a few old French authors that I return again and again; I only believe in French culture and regard everything in Europe that calls itself 'culture' as a misunderstanding, not to mention German culture.

The few instances of highly educated people I have encountered in Germany were of French origin, in particular Cosima Wagner, who as far as I am concerned was by far the leading voice in matters of taste.

The fact that I do not read Pascal but that I *love* him, as the most instructive victim of Christianity – slowly murdered, first in body, then in mind, as the sum of the logic of the most horrific form of inhuman cruelty; that I have something of Montaigne's mischievousness in my spirit and, who knows?, perhaps in my body too; that my artist's taste cannot but defend men like Molière, Corneille and Racine and this not entirely without wrath against a wild genius like Shakespeare – all this does not finally prevent me from regarding even the modern French writers as charming company. I cannot imagine any other century in history in which such a group of inquisitive yet subtle psychologists could have been gathered than in present-day Paris. Randomly, since their number is by no means small. I name Paul Bourget, Pierre Loti, Gyp, Meilhac, Anatole France, Jules Lemaître, or, singling out one of strong race, a genuine Latin of whom I am particularly fond, Guy de Maupassant. Between ourselves, I prefer *this* generation even to their great masters since they have all been corrupted by German philosophy (Taine for instance by Hegel, whom he has to thank for misunderstanding great men and times). Wherever Germany reaches out to, she *corrupts* culture. It was the war that 'redeemed' the spirit of France.

Stendhal (one of the happiest accidents of my life, for everything in it of lasting value came to me by chance, never because of recommendation) is invaluable with his anticipatory psychologist's eye, his grasp of facts, reminiscent of the greatest of all masters (Napoleon); and last but not least as an honest atheist, a rare figure in France, almost impossible to find – with all due respect to Prosper Mérimée… Perhaps I am myself jealous of Stendhal? He has taken the best atheist joke I could possibly have made away from me: 'God's only excuse is that he does not exist'… I myself have said somewhere: What was hitherto the greatest objection to life? *God*…'

4.

IT WAS Heinrich Heine who defined the meaning of a lyrical poet for me. In vain do I search all areas throughout the past millennia for a similarly sweet and passionate music. He possessed that divine wickedness without which I cannot image perfection; I assess men and races according to how closely they associate god with Satyr – and how they handle the German language! One day it will be said that Heine and I were by far the top jugglers of the German language, infinitely outstripping everything ordinary Germans could do with it.

I must be closely related to *Byron's* Manfred: I found all these abysses in my own soul – at the mere age of thirteen I was ready to read this work. I have nothing to say, just a contemptuous glance for those who dare to speak of Faust in the same breath as Manfred. The Germans are *incapable* of any notion of greatness: look at Schumann. Angry with this sickly Saxon, I actually composed a counter-overture to Manfred, of which Hans von Bülow declared he had never seen the like before: raping the muse of music, that's what it is, he said.

Searching for the best formula to do Shakespeare justice, I only ever come up with: 'He conceived the character of Caesar.' You cannot conjecture a thing like that – you either are him or you are not. The great poet *only* draws from his own experience – up to the point where he cannot bear to look at his own work later on. Whenever I reread my *Zarathustra* I must pace to and fro in my room for half an hour, unable to control my sobs.

I know of no more heartbreaking literature than that of Shakespeare: how he must have suffered to need to play the clown so badly; do you understand *Hamlet*? It is not doubt, but *certainty* that drives you mad... But to feel like that you must be deep, must be abysmal, must be a philosopher... We are all *afraid* of the truth... And let me tell you this: I know instinctively for certain that Lord Bacon is the originator, the self-torturer, of this most sinister type of literature: why should *I* bother about the pitiful chattering of American blockheads and half-wits? But the power for the greatest visionary realism is not only compatible with the greatest strength for action, with the monstrous, the crime – *it actually anticipates it*... We don't by far know enough about Lord Bacon, the first realist in the very sense of the word, to know *everything* he did, *everything* he aimed for, how he himself felt about *everything*... You critics can all go to hell! If I had called my Zarathustra something else, Richard Wagner for example, the acumen of two millennia would not have been enough to divine that the author of *Human, All Too Human* is the inventor of Zarathustra...

5.

WHILE SPEAKING of the recreational pursuits of my life I need to express my gratitude for him who afforded me by far the deepest and dearest forms of escape. This has been without doubt my intimate relationship with Richard Wagner. All other human relationships were fair enough; but I would not miss the days in Tribschen from my life – days of trust, of happiness, of marvellous opportunities and above all – of *deep* moments... I do not know what others made of Wagner, but nothing ever cast a cloud over *our* friendship.

This brings me back to France – I cannot give any reasons, I can only contemptuously pucker my mouth when I look to Wagnerians and their ilk, who think they honour Wagner by believing him to be like *themselves*... Since I am what I am, instinctively alienated from all things German (to the point that the mere presence of a German will make me constipated), the first meeting with Wagner was also my first sigh of relief ever. I felt him, I revered him as a *foreigner*, as the antithesis of, and a living protest against, all 'German virtues'.

We, who were children in the stagnant air of the 1850s, are necessarily pessimists with regard to the notion of

'German'; we cannot be anything else but revolutionaries – we will not accept any condition in which a *creep* will be at the top. I am totally oblivious to his attire – whether he is robed in scarlet or puts on a uniform. Well then! Wagner was a revolutionary – he ran away from the Germans...

The *artist* has no home in Europe except in Paris; the predilection for all the five senses which is a condition of Wagner's art, that sensitivity to nuance, the psychological morbidity, these can only be found in Paris. Nowhere else is there this passion for form, this seriousness about stage-setting, which is Parisian seriousness par excellence. The Germans have no idea of the extraordinary ambition that lives in the soul of a Parisian artist... Germans are good-natured – Wagner was certainly not... But I have already written enough on the subject of Wagner, where he stands, where he comes from (see *Beyond Good and Evil*, 'Aphorism 2'): it is the late French Romanticists, that high-flying and heaven-aspiring bunch of artists like Delacroix and Berlioz, who are essentially sick, terminally so, pure fanatics of *expression*, virtuosos to the last... Who was the first *intelligent* follower of Wagner, pray? Charles Baudelaire, the very man who first understood Delacroix, that archetypal Decadent in whom a whole generation of artists has recognized itself – perhaps he was also the last...

What was it that I could not forgive Wagner for? That he *condescended* to the Germans – that he became a German Imperialist... Whoever Germany reaches out to – she will *corrupt* their culture.

6.

ALL THINGS CONSIDERED, I would never have survived my youth without Wagner's music. For I was *condemned* to live amongst Germans. If you wish to escape from unbearable oppression, you need Hashish. Well then, I needed Wagner. Wagner is the antidote to everything essentially German, but it is a poison nevertheless, I do not deny it. As soon as there was a piano arrangement of *Tristan* available (thank you, Mr von Bülow), I was a Wagnerite. The older works of Wagner, I felt, were beneath me, they were too common, too 'German'... But to this day I am looking for works of a similar dangerous fascination to *Tristan*, that horrifying yet sweet quality of infinity. I am searching among all the arts, but in vain. All the mysteries of Leonardo da Vinci are forgotten at the first note of *Tristan*. It is absolutely the very highest point in Wagner's work, he recovered from it with the *Mastersingers* and the *Ring* cycle. To recuperate – that is a retrograde step in a nature like that of Wagner...

I thank my lucky stars that I lived at the right time and in particular amongst Germans, to have been able to appreciate this work – that is how strongly the curiosity of a psychologist has a hold on me. The world must be a poor place for those that have never been sick enough for the 'salaciousness of hell'; it is permissible, almost imperative to use a mystic formula here.

I believe that I know better than anyone else the prodigious feats of which Wagner is capable, the fifty worlds of unknown ecstasies to which only he could soar. Strong as I am now and able to use even the most dubious and dangerous

things to my advantage to become even more powerful, I see
Wagner as the great benefactor of my life. We are related in
that we suffered more than any other men of this century,
even made each other suffer, and that will bring together our
names once again for all eternity. For, just as Wagner as a
German is simply a misconception, so surely am I and always
will be. Two hundred years of psychological and artistic
discipline are required, my dear Germans... But it is all too
late...

7.

ONE MORE WORD for my most select readers: what do I
actually ask of music? It should be bright yet profound, like an
October's afternoon; it should be individual, carefree, tender,
like a dainty, sweet woman full of mischief and grace... I
will never accept that Germans *can* know the meaning of
music. The musicians generally accepted as Germans are all
foreigners: Slavs, Croats, Italians, Dutchmen or Jews; or else
they are Germans of a strong race now *extinct*, like Heinrich
Schütz, Bach and Handel. I myself am still enough of a Pole
to give up all the music in the world for that of Chopin. I
would make three exceptions here: with Wagner's *Siegfried
Idyll* and perhaps with some works of Liszt too, who with
his noble orchestration has the advantage over all other
musicians; and finally also with all those that grew up beyond
the Alps – *my side*... I would not miss Rossini for the world,
even less my Southern counterpart in music, my Venetian
maestro, Pietro Gasti. And when I say beyond the Alps, I
really only mean Venice. Whenever I want to find another

word for music, I inevitably come to say Venice. I do not know the difference between tears and music; I cannot think of joy or the *South* without the tremble of real fear.

> On the bridge I stood
> in recent muggy night,
> from afar a song
> came: like golden drops
> across the trembling rim.
> Gondolas, lights, music
> drunkenly they swam far into the dusk
>
> My soul, strings finely tuned,
> sang a boating song
> invisibly moved,
> secretly along,
> trembling in bright bliss
> – was someone listening in?

8.

IN ALL THIS – in the choice of food, location, climate and recreation – the instinct for self-preservation dominates, expressing itself most obviously as an instinct for *self-defence*. Not to see, not to hear most things, but to keep them at arm's length – this is the foremost prudence, the first evidence that you are not here by chance but out of necessity. The common word for this instinct of self-defence is *taste*. It is imperative not just to say 'no' where a 'yes' would be an act of 'unselfishness', but also to say *'no' as little as possible*.

Depart, detach yourself from situations where again and again it would be necessary to say 'no'. That is because the discharge of defensive energy, however slight, regular and habitual it has become, causes an extraordinary and absolutely superfluous loss. Our *greatest* energy discharge consists of the most frequent small ones. The defence, the keeping-at-arm's-length is a discharge – and make no mistake here – of strength *wasted* for negative ends. Simply by being constantly on your guard, you can become weak enough not to be able to defend yourself any longer.

Suppose I were to step out of my house and, instead of the quiet and noble city of Turin, were to encounter a provincial German town: why, my instinct would have to shut down, to repress everything that would force itself upon it from this downtrodden and cowardly world. Or if I were to find a German metropolis, this structure of vice in which nothing grows but where everything, good or bad, has been forcibly imported. What choice would I have then but to become a *hedgehog*? – But to have quills is a sheer waste, a twofold luxury even if I choose not to have quills but *open* hands instead...

Another form of prudence and self-defence is to react as *seldom as possible* and to avoid situations and conditions where you are condemned, as it were, to suspend your 'liberty' and initiative and become a mere bundle of reactions. For example, when we are dealing with books. The scholar who actually does little else but pore over books (he reads on average 200 books a day), in the end loses all his ability to think for himself. If he does not pore, he does not think! Whenever he thinks, he *answers* to a stimulus (a thought he has read) – and finally all he does is react. The scholar devotes all his energy to affirming or denying or reviewing all that has already been thought – he no longer thinks for himself... His instinct for self-defence has become brittle, otherwise he would defend himself against books. The scholar is a Decadent. I have seen it with my own eyes: gifted, generous and free-spirited natures, no more than thirty and already 'wrecks' from too much reading; nothing but matchsticks that you have to strike so that they emit a spark or 'thought'.

To read a *book* first thing in the morning at daybreak, at the dawn of your strength – that I call a vice!

9.

AT THIS POINT a direct answer to the question *how we become what we are* can no longer be evaded. And with that I touch upon the master stroke of the art of self-preservation – *Selfishness*... Let us assume that our task, the purpose, the *destiny* of the task exceeds by far an average norm, then there could be no greater danger but to come face-to-face *with* this task. To become what you are presupposes that you do not have the remotest idea *what* you are. From this point of view, even the *blunders* in your life have a unique meaning and value, the occasional deviation or straying from the path, the hesitations, the 'modesties', the seriousness, wasted upon tasks that are beyond *the* main task. This outlines a great prudence, possibly even the highest prudence; whereas 'Know Yourself' would be a sure way to lead to downfall, to forget yourself, to *misunderstand* yourself, to belittle yourself, to limit and moderate yourself becomes reason itself. In moral terms:

neighbourly love and living for others and other things *may* be the means of protection to maintain the most rigorous egoism. This is the exception where I, against all my self-imposed rules and conviction, take the part of the 'selfless' instincts: here they are engaged in the service of *egoism* and *self-discipline*.

The whole surface of consciousness (for consciousness is a surface) has to be kept free of any of the great imperatives. Beware even of every striking word or gesture! They all endanger the instinct to 'know itself' too soon. Meanwhile the organizing 'idea', destined to rule, continues to grow below; it becomes commanding; it leads you slowly *back* from deviations and aberrations; it prepares *individual* qualities and capacities that may one day be indispensable as the means to the whole – gradually, it develops all *serviceable* faculties before it indicates any trace of the dominant task of 'goal', 'purpose' and 'meaning'.

Viewed from this angle, my life is simply amazing. The task to *re-evaluate all values* required perhaps more abilities than could ever be found combined in one individual, and above all, also contrasting abilities that would at the same time not be mutually inimical, if not destructive. The ranking of abilities, distancing, the art of separating without creating hostility, to confuse nothing, to 'reconcile' nothing, to be enormously diverse yet the opposite of chaos – all this was the main condition and the long secret workings and artistic nature of my instinct. Its superior *guardianship* was so strong that at no time could I have any notion of what was growing within me – suddenly all my abilities *burst forth*: ripe and absolutely perfect. I fail to remember ever having exerted myself; there is truly no trace of a *struggle* in my life; I am the opposite of a heroic character. To 'want' something, to 'strive' for something, to focus on a 'purpose' or a 'wish', all these things I do not know from experience. Even at this moment I look out upon my future – a *wide* future – as upon a calm sea; there is no foam of desire upon it. I have not the slightest wish that anything should change from the way it is; I myself do not wish to change. But I have always been like that. I never wished for anything. I am someone who can say at the age of forty-four that he was never interested in *honours*, *women* or *money*. Not that these things were lacking… For instance, one fine day I found myself to be a university professor! I never even thought about it; after all, I was only twenty-four years old. In the same way, only two years earlier I suddenly was a philologist, in the sense that my *first* philological work, my beginning in every sense, was required by my teacher Ritschl to be printed in his magazine *Rheinisches Museum*. (*Ritschl* – I say it full of veneration – was the only genial scholar whom I have ever met. He possessed that pleasant notoriety that distinguishes us Thuringians and that makes even a German a nice person – we prefer to use secret and hidden paths to get to the truth. These words should not be taken as a slur upon my fellow countryman, the *intelligent* Leopold von Ranke.)

10.

AT THIS POINT you may ask me why I actually told you all these trivial and on the whole irrelevant details; I would seem to be harming my own cause, all the more so since I claim to represent great tasks. Let me say this to you: such small things as diet, location, climate, recreation, the whole casuistry of self-love, are by far more important than anything else that has been hitherto considered essential by us. Here in particular, we have to start to *rethink*. All those things that mankind has until now thought about with such earnestness are not even realities; they are mere fancies, indeed *lies*, arising from the bad instincts of sick and in the truest sense harmful natures: such concepts as 'god', 'soul', 'virtue', 'sin', 'the hereafter', 'truth', 'eternal life'... And yet we looked for the greatness of human nature, its 'divinity' in them... All questions of politics, of the social order, of education have been thoroughly falsified because the most harmful people were accepted by us as great men, by being taught to despise the so-called 'trivial' matters, which are really the fundamental concerns of life... Our current culture is highly ambiguous... The German emperor is in league with the Pope, as if the Pope was not the representative of the mortal enemy of life! What has been built today will not stand three years from now.

If I put my abilities to the test, never mind that what follows, a regime change or a new development as never seen before, I more than any other mortal can claim to be great. If I now compare myself with those people who were hitherto considered the 'first' among men, the difference becomes tangible. I do not even count these so-called 'first' men among human beings – for me they are the waste product of mankind, fiends deformed by disease and instincts of revenge; they are all monsters, rotten to the core and sick beyond cure, avenging themselves on life... I choose to be their very opposite. It is my prerogative to be highly sensitive to any indication of healthy instincts. There is not a single morbid trait in me; even during my long and serious illness I have never become morbid. You will look in vain for a trace of fanaticism in my character. No-one is able to point out even a single instance in my life where I was presumptuous or pathetic. The pathos of gestures is *not* part of greatness; whoever needs gestures is *false*... Beware of the picturesque!

Life became easiest for me whenever it demanded the most from me. Those who saw me during the seventy days of this autumn when, without interruption, I performed so many things of the first order that no-one can match it or do better, things that will be representative for centuries to come, will not have noticed a single sign of tension in me, but rather my exuberant wellbeing and cheerfulness.

Never did I eat with greater enjoyment, never did I sleep better. I know no better means to deal with great tasks but *play*; this is an essential prerequisite and a sign of greatness. The slightest constraint, a gloomy expression, any harsh sound from the throat are all objections to a person, but how much more so to his work!... We must have no nerves... Even to *suffer* from loneliness is an objection – I personally have only ever suffered from being 'crowded out'.

At an absurdly young age, when I was only seven, I already knew that I could never be stirred by human speech. Did anyone see me sad because of it? Today, I still feel the same affability towards everyone, I give my attention even to the most lowly born, and in all this there is not an ounce of arrogance or contempt. Those whom I despise will soon *know* that I despise them, my mere existence angers those with bad blood in them. My formula for greatness in man is to *embrace your destiny*, to alter nothing, either in the future, or in the past, or in all eternity. Do not simply endure necessity and even less, hide it, but *love* it – all idealism is a falsehood in the face of necessity.

Chapter 3

Why I write such excellent books

1.

I AM ONE THING, my books are another... Before I talk about them, I would like to touch upon the question about whether or *not* they are understood. I do it as casually as is fitting, since the time for this question has not yet come, really. For me, too, the time has not yet come, some of us are born posthumously.

One day, there will have to be institutions where men can live and teach as I myself know how to live and teach: perhaps then they will also establish professorships for the interpretation of *Zarathustra*. But I would be completely contradicting myself, if I expected ears *and hands* for my truths today. Not only does it seem understandable that no-one listens to me yet, that no-one knows what to do with me, it also seems to me quite right that it is so. I do not wish to be taken for someone else – and I too must not take myself for someone else.

Let me say it once again, there have been very few instances of 'ill will' in my life, even less of literary 'ill will'. However, there have been far too many of *pure stupidity*... To pick up a book of mine seems to me to be one of the rarest honours man can pay himself – I even assume he takes his shoes off first, or his boots… When Doctor Heinrich von Stein once seriously complained not to have understood a single word of my *Zarathustra*, I told him that that was as it should be: to have understood just six sentences or better; to have *lived* them, would lift a man on to a higher level among mortals than 'modern man' could reasonably hope for. How *could* I, with *this* feeling for distance, even wish to be read by 'modern men' as I know them! My triumph is precisely the opposite to that of Schopenhauer's 'read and be read' – I say, 'I am not read, I shall not read.'

Not that I wish to underestimate the fun that I had when I met with the *innocence* of people saying no to my books. Even this very summer, at a time when I could perhaps upset the apple cart of all literature together with my weighty, far too weighty literature, a professor from Berlin University told me good-naturedly that I should find a new form of writing: nobody would read anything like that.

In the end it was not Germany but Switzerland that came up with the two most extreme cases: an essay by a Dr V Widman in the Bernese newspaper *Bund* about *Beyond Good and Evil* as 'Nietzsche's dangerous book' and a general account about all my books by a Mr Karl Spitteler in the very same newspaper are the highlight of my life – I shall not say why… The latter spoke of my *Zarathustra* as 'an advanced *exercise in style*', for example, and suggested I should also try and add some substance. Dr Widman expressed his respect for the courage of my endeavour to abolish all decent feelings.

Thanks to a little trick of chance, every sentence here was, with admirable consistency, a truth stood on its head: at bottom there was nothing else to do but to 're-evaluate values', to hit the nail on the head as far as I was concerned in a remarkable fashion – instead of hitting my head with a nail. I shall try to explain myself all the more.

In the end, no-one can learn any more from matters, books included, than he already knows. Without access to events, you will not have an ear for them. Let us take an extreme case and suppose a book contains only events that lie entirely outside the range of general or even less general experiences and suppose it is the first language for a new series of experiences. In such a case nothing really will be heard at all and thanks to an acoustic delusion, you will think that since you hear nothing *there is nothing there.* This, at least, is my usual experience, and proves, if you like, the *originality* of my experience. Whoever thought they had understood something in my work will have appropriated something from it in his own image – quite often the opposite of me, for instance an 'idealist'; whoever understood nothing I wrote will deny that I am worth considering at all.

The word '*Superman*' as a definition of a type of greatest perfection in contrast to 'modern' man or 'good' man, to Christians and other nihilists – a word that in the mouth of Zarathustra, the *destroyer* of morality, acquires a very profound meaning – was in all innocence understood almost everywhere in the light of those values that the figure of Zarathustra stood against – I mean as an 'idealistic' type of higher human being – half 'saint', half 'genius'… Other learned cattle have accused me of Darwinism because of this definition; it was even seen as belonging to that 'hero cult' of Carlyle's, that great unconscious and involuntary swindler, which was so maliciously rejected by me. Once I whispered in someone's ear he should look to Cesare Borgia rather than Parsifal and he could not believe his ears.

You must forgive me my lack of any curiosity as far as reviews of my books are concerned, in particular when they appear in newspapers. My friends and publishers know this and do not mention them to me. In one particular case, however, I once found out about all the sins committed against one of my books – it was *Beyond Good and Evil*. I could tell a pretty story about that. Would you believe that the *Nationalzeitung* (a Prussian newspaper – this information is for my readers from abroad; I myself read only the *Journal des Débats*) in all seriousness regarded this book as a 'sign of the times', a piece of right and proper *Junker philosophy*, which its organ the *Kreuz* newspaper simply lacked the courage to come up with?

2.

THIS WAS MENTIONED for the benefit of Germans, for I have readers everywhere – all highly educated minds, characters in top positions and with great responsibilities on their shoulders; among my readers are even some true geniuses. In Vienna, in St Petersburg, in Stockholm, in Copenhagen, in Paris and in New York – everywhere I have been discovered, but *not* in Europe's plain country: in Germany… And let me be honest, I am even happier about my non-readers, those that have neither heard my name nor of the word 'philosophy', but wherever I go, here in Turin for instance, all faces light up and soften. The thing that so far has flattered me most is that old peddler women will not rest until they have picked for me the very sweetest bunch from amongst their grapes. *For this* you must be a philosopher.

Not for nothing are the Poles called the Frenchmen of the Slavs. A lovely Russian woman will not mistake my origins for a moment. I am no use at being pompous; at best I can go as far as embarrassment… To think in German, to feel in German – I can do it all, but *that* is too much for me… My former tutor Ritschl went so far as to say that I planned even my philological treatises like a Parisian novelist – that they were absurdly thrilling. In Paris itself people are surprised about '*toutes mes audaces et finesses*' – to quote Monsieur Taine; I am afraid that even in the highest forms of the dithyramb, the hymn of praise to Dionysus, you will find traces of that ingredient that can never be stupid, never be 'German' – it is called 'wit'… I can do no other, so help me God! Amen. We all know, some even know from experience, what a long-ear is. Well, I dare to assert that I have the tiniest ears. This is of no little interest to the ladies – am I right that they feel understood by me?… I am the supreme *anti-ass* and as such a world-historical beast – I am in Greek, and not only in Greek, the *Antichrist*…

3.

I KNOW on the whole my privileges as a writer; in a few cases I was even assured how much the habitual reading of my books would 'ruin' the taste buds. It is simply unbearable to read any other books, least of all philosophical ones. It is a distinction beyond all comparison to enter this elegant and delicate world – you certainly do not need to be a German; it is in short a distinction that must be earned. Anyone, however, akin to me in *loftiness* of will, experiences the true ecstasies of learning by reading them: for I swoop from heights where no bird ever flew, I know abysses where no foot ever lost its footing. I was told it was not possible to put any book of mine down – even that I disturbed a good night's sleep… There is absolutely no prouder or at the same time more subtle kind of book: it achieves here and there the highest that can be achieved on earth, cynicism; you have to conquer it with the most delicate fingerstrokes, using them like the most valiant fists. Every weakness of the soul will bar you from it for good and ever, even a belly-ache; you do not need nerves but you have to have a cheerful abdomen. Not just poverty, the stuffy air in a soul excludes you from it, but much more so cowardice, the unclean and the secret longing for revenge deep down in the bowels: one word from me drives all bad instincts into full view. Among my acquaintances are several test animals, which I use to sample their very varied and instructive reactions to my books. Those who wish to have nothing to do with their contents, my so-called friends for example, become 'impersonal', they wish me luck to have 'done it once again' – apparently there is improvement because of a happier ring to the books… These completely reprobate 'spirits', these 'beautiful souls', liars all in the extreme, have absolutely no idea what to do with these books – therefore they feel they are *beneath* them – a consistent reaction of all 'beautiful souls'. The cattle among my acquaintances, the mere Germans, if you don't mind my saying so, let me know that they are not always of my opinion but that they agree here and there, for instance… I have heard this even with regard to my *Zarathustra*.

Similarly, every 'feminist' in a person, even in a man, closes the gate as far as I am concerned: never will you enter the labyrinth of daring knowledge. You have to be completely ruthless with yourself, must be used to great *hardness*, to remain cheerful and merry among all these implacable truths. If I conjure up the picture of a perfect reader, he always becomes a monster of courage and curiosity, yet also of subtlety, cunning and prudence – a born adventurer and explorer. After all, I can not describe any better than *Zarathustra* did *who* I am actually addressing: those few he was prepared to reveal his riddle to.

'To you, you bold explorers and experimenters and who ever else embarked beneath cunning sails on dreadful seas,

– to you, you drunk, with riddles revelling in twilight, whose souls are being lured by flutes down every treacherous abyss,

– for you do not want to grope your way along a thread with a coward's hand, and where you are able to *divine*, you hate to *open up*...'

4.

AT THE SAME TIME, I wish to make a general comment about my *art of style*. The meaning of every style is to *communicate* a state of mind, an inner tension of pathos through symbols, including the timing of these symbols – that is the character of every style; and in view of the fact that the multitude of states of mind in me is enormous, I have also many styles at my disposal – in short, the most diverse art of style that ever was available to man. Any style is *good* which genuinely communicates a state of mind, which does not make a mistake when using symbols, the timing of symbols, and the *moods* – all phrasing is to do with creating moods. Here my instinct is impeccable.

Good style *in itself* is a folly, mere 'idealism' or 'beautiful *in itself*' for instance, or 'goodness *in itself*' or 'the thing *itself*'… This is assuming that there are ears to hear – that they are *capable* and worthy of such pathos, that there are still plenty who are *worth* communicating with… Meanwhile my Zarathustra, for example, is still searching for such people – ah, he will have to go looking for a long time yet! – You have to *deserve* to listen to him… And until then, there will be nobody who will understand the *art* that has been squandered here. No-one else has lavished newer, more extraordinary, more genuinely original forms of art on to the world. That this was possible in the German language had yet to be substantiated; I myself would have dismissed it most emphatically. Before me, nobody knew what the German language was capable of – what any language is capable of.

The art of *grand* rhythm and *grand style* of phrasing, expressing a tremendous swing in sublime and superhuman passion, was first discovered by me: with a hymn of praise entitled 'The Seven Seals' which is the last discourse of the third part of *Zarathustra*. With that I soared thousands of miles above everything which hitherto has been called poetry.

5.

THE FACT that my books are written by a psychologist, unparalleled in history, is perhaps the first impression a good reader may get, a reader such as I deserve, and one who reads me as the good old philologists used to read their Horace. Those doctrines that are really accepted by all the world, not to speak of the la-di-da philosophers, moralists and other blockheads and cabbages, seem to me but naive blunders – for example that belief that 'altruistic' and 'egoistic' are opposites, while the ego itself is merely a 'supreme swindle', an 'ideal'… There are *no such things* as egoistic or altruistic deeds: both terms are a psychological nonsense. Or the proposition 'man strives for happiness'… or 'happiness is the reward of virtue'… or 'joy and misery are opposite values'… Morality, the femme fatale, has falsified all psychology and *outmoralized* it until only that horrible humbug that love must be 'altruistic' was left… You have to have a firm grip of *yourself*, stand steadfastly on both legs, otherwise you *cannot* love at all. Women know that all too well: they don't give a damn for unselfish and merely objective men… May I dare to say that I know women? That this is part of my Dionysian heritage? Who knows, perhaps I am the first psychologist of the eternal-feminine. They all love me – which is old hat (not counting the damaged, the 'emancipated' ones, who haven't got what it takes to have children). Luckily I am not willing to let myself be torn to bits – your typical woman tears those she loves to bits… I know these amiable maenads… Oh, what a dangerous, sly, subterranean little beast she is! And at the same time so lovely!… A little woman pursuing her revenge would even destroy fate.

Woman is inexpressibly more wicked than man, but also cleverer. Goodness in a woman is already a form of *degeneration*… A so-called 'beautiful soul' in a woman is essentially a physiological disease – I shall not go any further, otherwise this would become a medical discourse. The struggle for *equal* rights is actually a symptom of disease; every doctor knows it. Women, the more feminine they are, fight with all their might against rights in general: the natural order of things, in the eternal *war* between the sexes she always has the greatest advantage.

Have you ever listened to my definition of love? It is the only one worthy of a philosopher. Love is conducted like war because it is at heart the deadly hatred of the sexes. Have you heard my reply to the question of how a woman can be *cured*, saved? Give her a child. Women need children, to her a man is merely a means to an end: thus spoke Zarathustra.

'The emancipation of woman' is the instinctive hatred of the *misshapen* – that is to say, infertile – women for her fertile sisters; the fight against 'man' is only ever a means, an excuse, a strategy. In raising themselves to the level of 'women *per se*', of 'supreme woman', of 'ideal woman', they try to bring down the general level of women's rank; and there is no surer way of doing so than higher education, wearing trousers and the voting rights of cattle. To tell the truth, the emancipated are the *anarchists* in the world of the 'eternal-feminine', the failures and losers whose lowest instinct is revenge... A whole species of the ugliest type of 'idealism', incidentally, can also be found among men; for instance with Henrik Ibsen, that typical old maid, it is aimed at *poisoning* the clear conscience and the natural spirit in sexual love... And not to leave any doubt about my heartfelt and strict views on these matters I will give you another clause from my code of morality against *vice*: I use the word 'vice' to fight any form of perversion, but if you prefer a finer word, use 'idealism'. The clause reads: 'Preaching of chastity is a public incitement to perverse acts. All contempt for sexual matters, all sullying of them by applying the concept "unclean" is itself a crime against life – it is the actual crime against the holy spirit of life.'

6.

TO GIVE YOU an idea of my role as a psychologist, I give you a curious bit of psychological analysis from my book *Beyond Good and Evil* – but I forbid any conjectures as to whom I may or may not describe in this passage.

'The Genius of the heart, as that great recluse possesses it, the divine tempter and born pied piper of consciences, whose voice is able to descend right down into the underworld of every soul, who does not speak a word or cast a glance without some seductive power or trick, whose exquisite skill enables him to seem, not what he is but what is to those who follow him yet *one more* compulsion to press ever closer to him, to follow him ever more enthusiastically and wholeheartedly... The genius of the heart, who makes all loud and self-satisfied things fall silent and listen out, who smoothes the rough souls and lets them taste a new longing: to lie still, like a mirror, that the low sky may be reflected in them... The genius of the heart, who teaches the clumsy and over-hasty hand to hesitate and to grasp more tenderly, who senses the hidden and forgotten treasure, the drop of goodness and sweet spirituality beneath thick black ice and who is a divining rod for every grain of gold that was buried for years and years, imprisoned under heaps of mud and sand... The genius of the heart, whose very touch enriches everyone, not with gifts and surprises, not by the wealth and stealth of others, but richer in themselves, more aware of themselves than before, opened up, caressed and sounded out by a soft westerly wind, perhaps even less sure, more tender, more fragile, more broken, but full of hopes that have not yet a name, full of new will and flowing forth, full of new unwillingness and flowing back.'

THE BIRTH OF TRAGEDY.

1.

TO BE FAIR to *The Birth of Tragedy* (1872) we have to overlook a few things. Whatever was wrong with the book gave it its *effect* and fascination, that is to say its practical application to *Wagnerism* as if that were a symptom of an *ascent*. Because of it, this book was an event in Wagner's life; it was only from then on that the name of Wagner evoked great hopes. People still remind me of this today, occasionally even in the context of *Parsifal*, how it is really *my* fault that the movement became a *cult* and excited such high opinions.

I found on several occasions that the book was referred to as the 'Rebirth of Tragedy from the Spirit of Music'; people had only ears for a new formula for the art, the intention, the task of *Wagner,* and because of it they did not notice what was truly valuable in the book. 'Hellenism and Pessimism', that would have been a less ambiguous title, suggesting a first instruction of how the Greeks coped with pessimism – how they *overcame* it… Precisely their tragedies prove that the Greeks were *no* pessimists: Schopenhauer went wrong here, in precisely the same way as he went wrong in all other things.

If looked at with some degree of objectivity, *The Birth of Tragedy* seems anachronistic; you would never dream that it was *begun* amid the thunder of the Battle of Wörth. I have thought through these problems before the walls of Metz, on cold September nights while on duty as a medical orderly. The book seems to be some fifty years older than it really is. Politically it is indifferent, 'un-German' you would say today. It smells offensively of Hegel, but some of the formulas have the doleful whiff of Schopenhauer. It is a 'concept' – the antithesis of the Dionysian and the Apollonian translated into metaphysics; history itself is the development of this 'concept' whereby in tragedy this polarity has been sublimated into a unity. These things have never before faced each other and are now suddenly juxtaposed; they are used to illuminate each other and are now *comprehensible*… Opera, for example, and the revolution.

The two decisive *innovations* of the book are firstly that Greeks have understood the Dionysian phenomenon; for the first time a psychological analysis is given and it is considered to be the root of all Greek art. The other is the understanding of Socratism: Socrates is recognized for the first time as an instrument of Greek disintegration, as a typical Decadent. 'Rationality' *versus* instinct. 'Rationality' is at any price seen as a dangerous, life-undermining power.

On the matter of Christianity there is a profound and hostile silence throughout the book. It is neither Apollonian nor

Dionysian; it *denies* all *aesthetic* values – the only values that *The Birth of Tragedy* recognizes; it is nihilistic in its truest sense, while the ultimate limit of affirmation is attained in the Dionysian symbol. Once the Christian priests are even alluded to as a 'spiteful kind of dwarf' dwelling 'deep, deep beneath the earth'.

2.

THIS BEGINNING is strange beyond belief. As far as I know, I myself had *discovered* the only metaphor and counterpart in history, and thus I became the first to understand the amazing phenomenon of the Dionysian. Similarly, in recognizing Socrates as a Decadent, I could prove unequivocally how little the security of my psychological grasp would be endangered by any moral idiosyncrasy; regarding Morality itself as a symptom of decadence is an innovation and unique in the history of knowledge. How high had I jumped with these two insights above the wretched and shallow chatter about optimism versus pessimism. I was the first to see the actual polarity: the degenerating instinct that turns against life with subliminal vengefulness (Christianity, the philosophy of Schopenhauer, in a sense even the philosophy of Plato, the whole of idealism in its typical form) versus the formula of *supreme affirmation* born out of abundance, of profusion, to say 'yes' without reserve, say 'yes' to suffering itself, to guilt, to all that is dubious and strange in existence itself… This ultimate, most joyous, most wantonly extravagant 'yes' to life is not just the ultimate insight, it is also the *most profound*, the one most strongly confirmed and upheld by truth and science. Nothing needs to be taken away, nothing is superfluous – as it is, the aspects of existence rejected by the

Christians and other nihilists are of an infinitely higher order in the hierarchy of values than even that which the instinct of decadence could approve of. To understand this requires *courage* and, as a condition for that, an excess of *strength*; for precisely as far as courage *may* dare to go governed by precisely that strength, you will come closer to the truth. Knowledge, saying 'yes' to reality, is just as necessary for the strong as cowardice and the *flight* from reality – the 'ideal' – is for the weak, who are inspired by weakness... It is not given to them to know that the Decadents *need* the lie, it is one of the conditions for their survival.

Whoever does not merely understand the word 'Dionysian' but sees *himself* described by the word 'Dionysian' has no need to refute Plato or Christianity or Schopenhauer – he can *smell the decay.*

3.

I FINALLY explained in my book *The Twilight of the Idols* the extent to which I have discovered the concept of the 'tragic', the ultimate knowledge of the psychology of tragedy. 'Saying "Yes" to life even with its most alien and difficult problems; the will to live rejoicing in its own boundlessness even while *sacrificing* its most superior types – *that* is what I called Dionysian, that was how I saw the bridge to the psychology of the *tragic* poet. *Not* to be rid of fear and pity, not to purge myself of a dangerous effect by its vehement discharge as Aristotle misunderstood it, but the eternal joy of becoming in itself beyond all fear and pity, that joy that included even *joy in destroying.*'

In this sense I have the right to see myself as the first *tragical philosopher* – that is to say, the extreme antithesis and polar opposite of a pessimistic philosopher. Before I came along, this translation of the Dionysian into philosophical pathos did not exist: *the tragic wisdom was lacking* – I looked in vain for signs of it even among the *great* Greeks of philosophy, those that lived two centuries before Socrates. I retained some doubt in the case of Heraclitus, in whose presence I felt altogether warmer and more comfortable then anywhere else. The affirmative answer to death *and destruction*, which is the decisive feature of a Dionysian philosophy, saying 'yes' to opposition and war, of *becoming* along with radical rejection even of the concept of '*being*' – all this is definitively more closely related to me than anything else thought to date. The doctrine of the 'eternal recurrence', that is to say of the unconditional and infinite circuit of all things – this doctrine of Zarathustra *could* already have been taught by Heraclitus. Stoicism, having inherited almost all their fundamental ideas of Heraclitus, shows traces of it.

4.

THIS BOOK offers tremendous hope. Ultimately, I have no reason to withdraw the hope for a Dionysian future from music. Let us look a century ahead and assume that my assault on two thousand years of unnaturalness and abuse of mankind is successful. That new denomination of life, which takes the greatest of all tasks, the advancement of mankind, into its hands, including the merciless destruction of all that is degenerative and parasitic, will make that *abundance of life* on earth (from which the Dionysian state must also grow again) once again possible. I promise a *tragic age*: the greatest art of saying 'Yes' to life, tragedy itself, will be reborn when mankind has weathered the recognition of the hardest but most necessary war *without suffering on its account...*

A psychologist might still add that the Wagnerian music I heard in my youth had absolutely nothing to do with Wagner, that when I described the Dionysian music I described what *I* had heard – that I instinctively had to translate and transfigure everything into the new spirit that I had within me. The evidence for that, *as convincing as any evidence can be*, is my essay 'Wagner in Bayreuth' – all psychologically decisive passages only speak of me, you can happily insert my name or the word 'Zarathustra' whenever the text mentions Wagner. The entire picture of the artist *in praise of Dionysus* is the picture of the *pre-existent* poet of Zarathustra, sketched with incredible profundity and without touching in the slightest on Wagnerian reality. Wagner himself was aware of that; he did not recognize himself in this essay.

Similarly, 'the idea of Bayreuth' was transformed into something that is no mystery to those who know my Zarathustra: into that *great noon*, at which the most select will consecrate themselves for the greatest of all tasks. Who can say? The vision of a feast I shall yet live to see... The pathos of the first pages is world-historical; the *glance* spoken of on the seventh page is Zarathustra's distinctive glance; Wagner, Bayreuth, the whole provincial German wretchedness are a cloud in which an infinite mirage of the future is reflected. Even psychologically all decisive traits of my own nature are projected into that of Wagner, the side-by-side proximity of the brightest and the most calamitous forces, the will to power as no man ever possessed it before, the ruthless bravery in the spirit, the unlimited power to learn without suppressing the will to act. All in this essay is a prophetic announcement: the impending rebirth of the Greek spirit, the necessity of the new Alexanders who will *tie* the Gordian knot of Greek culture once again… Listen to the world-historical emphasis, with which the concept 'tragic attitude' is introduced at the end of section 4: this essay is full of world-historical emphasis. This is the most foreign sounding 'objectivity' possible: the absolute certainty about what I *am* projected on some chance reality – the truth about me spoken from some gruesome depth. At the beginning of section 9, the *style* of Zarathustra is described in dramatic detail and anticipated; and never will there be a more magnificent expression for the *event* of Zarathustra, an act of tremendous purification and consecration of humanity, than can be found in section 6.

The Untimely Meditations

1.

THE FOUR *Untimely Meditations* are by all means militant. They prove that I was not some 'Jack the dreamer' or fantasist but that I actually enjoy drawing a sword – or is it just that my wrists are dangerously flexible. The *first* assault (1873) was aimed at German culture upon which even then I looked down with merciless contempt, since it was without meaning, without substance and without aim: a mere 'public opinion'.

There is no more malignant error of judgement than to believe that the great military success of the Germans was to prove anything in favour of this culture – least of all *its* triumph over France... The *second* Meditation (1874) illuminates the dangerous element in how we make science operate, gnawing at life and poisoning it; life is made *sick* by this dehumanized grinding of gears and mechanism, the 'impersonality' of the worker, and the false economy of the 'division of labour'. The *aim* is lost; culture, ways and means, how modern methods of science are *barbarized*... This essay recognized for the first time that the 'sense of history' of which this century is so proud is a sickness, a typical symptom of decay. In the *third* and *fourth* Meditations two images of the most extreme *self-love* and *self-discipline* are offered in contrast as a pointer to a *higher* concept of culture; to restore the concept of culture – Schopenhauer and Wagner, *or*, in a word, Nietzsche. These untimely types are beyond comparison, since they are full of a sovereign contempt for all that surrounds them by the name of 'the German Empire', 'Culture', 'Christianity', 'Bismarck', 'Success'...

2.

OF THESE FOUR ATTACKS, the first was extraordinarily successful. The commotion it made was splendid in every sense. I had touched the sore point of a victorious nation – that their victory was *not* a cultural event but perhaps something entirely different... The response came from all sides, not just from the old friends of David Strauss whom I had ridiculed as the archetypal cultural philistine and self-satisfied ass, in short as the author of his beer-hall gospel *The Old and New*

Faith (the expression 'cultural philistine' taken from my essay has since become part of the German language). These old friends, citizens of Württemberg and Swabia, whom I deeply hurt by making fun of their prodigy, their Strauss, replied in as plain and uncouth a manner as I could have hoped for. The replies from Prussia were more prudent – after all, they were of true Prussian Blue. The rudest reply came from a Leipzig newspaper, the notorious *Grenzboten*. It caused me some difficulties to restrain the indignant Baselers from taking action. Only a few old gentlemen were unconditionally on my side, acting from mixed and often unfathomable motives. Ewald from Göttingen was one of them and he suggested that my assault had had fatal consequences for Strauss. Also the old Hegelian Bruno Bauer, who from then on was one of my most attentive readers. During his last years he liked to refer to me, for example, when giving von Treitschke, the Prussian historiographer, a steer on whom he might ask for information about the concept of 'culture', which he seemed to have lost. The most thoughtful, also the lengthiest comments about the essay and its author, come from an old disciple of the philosopher von Baader, a Professor Hoffmann from Würzburg. On reading my essay, he predicted a great destiny for me – bringing about a kind of crisis and ultimate decision with regard to the problem of atheism, whose most instinctive and ruthless convert he assumed me to be. It was atheism that led me to Schopenhauer.

By far the most acutely heard and most keenly felt was an extraordinarily strong and brave plea on my behalf by the usually very moderate Karl Hillebrand, this last *humane*

German with knowledge of how to put pen to paper. His piece was first published in the *Augsburger Zeitung*; these days you will find a somewhat amended version in his collected essays. He described the essay as an event, a turning point, a dawning of awareness, an excellent sign, as a *true* return of German earnestness and German passion for all things intellectual.

Hillebrand was full of praise for the style of the essay, for its maturity, for its perfect tact in distinguishing between the person and the issue; he honoured it by calling it the best polemical essay written in German – since the skill of polemics is so dangerous and inadvisable, in particular for Germans. Backing me up to the hilt, even intensifying the comments I had dared to make against the galloping barbarization of the German language ('these days they act the purist and can no longer form a sentence'), with the same contempt for the 'top writers' of this nation, he concluded with an expression of his admiration for my *courage*, that 'supreme courage which is determined to put the people's favourites in the dock'…

The effects of this essay are of almost incalculable value to my life. So far, nobody has tried to quarrel with it. There is a silence; in Germany I am treated with a certain gloomy caution: for years I have made use of an unconditional freedom of speech which today nobody, least of all in the German Empire, seems to be at *liberty* to do. My paradise lies in 'the shadow of my sword'… In all truth, I only put into practice one of Stendhal's principles: he advises us to enter any society with a *duel*. And how I had picked my opponent! The foremost German freethinker!… Indeed, an altogether new type of libertine spirit was expressed for a first time in this way; to this day nothing is more foreign and less related to me than the whole European and American species of '*libre penseur*'. I am much more thoroughly at odds with these incorrigible blockheads and fools and their 'modern ideas' than with any of their opponents. They also want in their way to 'improve' mankind in their own image; they would fight an irreconcilable war against what I am and what I *want*, if only they understood it – however, all of them still believe in the 'ideal'... I am the first *immoralist*.

3.

I CANNOT SAY that the *Untimely Meditations* with titles like 'Schopenhauer' or 'Wagner' would contribute much to an understanding or even just raise the relevant psychological questions in either case, give or take the odd exception. Thus, for example, the essay describes the elementary in Wagner's character with profound instinctive certainty as an actor's talent that only draws conclusions from its means and purposes. I did not really want to dwell on psychology in these essays but to pursue a unique problem of education, a new concept of *self-discipline*, *self-defence* to the point of hardness; a path to greatness and to world-historical tasks that must be expressed for a first time. Broadly speaking, I caught hold of two famous and as yet undiagnosed types, the way we grab an opportunity when it presents itself in order to say something; in order to have at hand a few more formulas, symbols, means of expression. This is finally, and with a wisdom that seems uncanny to me, suggested in section 7 in the third Untimely Meditation; Plato used Socrates in this way, as a sign language for Plato.

Now that I am looking back from some distance upon

the conditions which these essays bear witness to, I cannot deny that they speak really only of me. The essay 'Wagner in Bayreuth' is a vision of my future, but in 'Schopenhauer as Educator' I describe my innermost biography, my *becoming*. Above all, though, it was about my *promise*!... *What* I am today, *where* I am today (at a giddy height where I no longer speak with words but with lightning bolts) – how far away was I from this at the time!

But I *saw* the land; I did not deceive myself for a moment about the way, the sea, the danger – *and* the success! The great calm of the promise, this happy gaze into a future that should not remain just a promise! Here, every word is based on experience, is deep, is inward; the most painful is there too – it contains words that are virtually dripping with blood. But a wind of *great* freedom blows above it all; the wound itself is no objection.

I see the philosopher as a terrible explosive endangering everything. My concept of the 'philosopher' is worlds removed from any concept that would include even a Kant, not to mention the academic 'ruminants' and other professors of philosophy: this essay offers an invaluable lesson, even if it must be admitted that at bottom it is not 'Schopenhauer as Educator' but 'Nietzsche as Educator' who is speaking. Considering that in those days my trade was that of a scholar and perhaps that I was *good at it*, it is not entirely without significance that an austere sample of scholar-psychology suddenly reveals itself in this essay – it expresses the *feeling of distance*, the absolute certainty I felt about what was to be my life's work and what could be dismissed as just means to an end. I was clever enough to have been many things in many different places in order to make myself singular – to arrive at one thing. For a time I also *had* to become a scholar.

HUMAN, ALL TOO HUMAN.
WITH TWO SEQUELS

1.

HUMAN, ALL TOO HUMAN is the monument to a crisis. It calls itself a book for *free* spirits: almost every sentence marks some kind of victory – I liberated myself with it from anything in my nature that *does not belong*. Idealism does not belong to me – the title reads 'where *you* see ideal things, *I* see – the human, ah, the all too human!' I know mankind *better*… The term 'free spirit' cannot have any other meaning here but that it is *liberated*, a spirit that took control of itself once again. The tone, the sound of voice, has completely changed; you will find the book clever, detached, occasionally hard and mocking. A certain spirituality kept in *good* taste seems to maintain the upper hand over a more passionate undercurrent. In this context, the publication of the book in 1878 can actually be seen as an excuse to celebrate the hundredth anniversary of the death of Voltaire. For Voltaire, contrary to all those who wrote after him, was above all an aristocrat of the mind – just like me.

The name Voltaire on one of my essays – that really meant progress – *toward*s *me*… If you look more closely, you will discover a merciless spirit that knows all the hideouts of the ideal, where it has its secret dungeons and also therefore where it can still lurk in safety. With a torch in both hands (for once its light is steady), you will shine through the dark into this *underworld* of the ideal. This is war, but a war without gunpowder and smoke, without bellicose attitudes, without pathos and torn limbs – all that would still be 'idealism'. One mistake after another is calmly laid on ice, the ideal is not refuted – it simply *freezes to death*. Here, for example, the 'genius' freezes to death, a little further on it is the 'saint'; under a huge icicle the 'hero'; and in the end 'belief' freezes to death, the so-called 'conviction', 'pity' too cools down considerably – almost everywhere 'the matter in itself' freezes to death…

2.

THE BEGINNINGS of this book go right back to the weeks of the first Bayreuth festivals; a profound alienation from all that surrounded me there is one of its preconditions. Those who have any notion of the visions I had already encountered then can imagine how I felt, when one day I woke up in Bayreuth. It was as if in a dream… Where was I? I recognized nothing, I hardly recognized Wagner. In vain did I leaf through my memories: Tribschen, a distant island of the blessed – not a trace of similarity. The incomparable days when the foundation stone was laid, the small *elect* group of people that celebrated it and whose sensitivity I could take for granted – not a trace of similarity. *What had happened?* – They had translated Wagner into German! The Wagnerian had become Wagner's master!

German art! the *German* Master! *German* beer!… We others, who know only too well what subtle artist and what cosmopolitanism of taste is exclusively addressed by Wagner's art, were beside ourselves to find Wagner decorated with German 'virtues'. I understand, indeed, I know the Wagnerian;

I have 'experienced' three generations from the late Brendel onwards who confused Wagner with Hegel down to the 'idealists' of *Bayreuther Blätter* who confused Wagner with themselves. I have heard every kind of confession of 'beautiful souls' about Wagner. A kingdom for one sensible word!

In truth, a hair-raising company! All philistines and cabbages – endlessly charming! No deformed monster is missing, not even the anti-Semite. Poor Wagner! Where had he ended up – he would have been better off in a herd of swine! But among Germans!… For the instruction of future generations we should really take a true Bayreuth citizen, stuff him, or, even better, preserve him in surgical spirit since spirit is needed – with the label underneath reading, 'This is the "spirit" on which the German Empire is founded…'

Enough, I left in the midst of it all for a couple of weeks, very abruptly, even though a charming Parisian tried to console me. The only apology I offered Wagner was a fatalistic telegram. In a place called Klingenbrunn, hidden away in the deep Bohemian forest, I dragged a deep depression and contempt for the Germans around like a sickness *and* from time to time I would write a sentence or two in my notebook, under the general title 'The Ploughshare', aphorisms of strong psychological content that may perhaps still be found in *Human, All Too Human*.

3.

WHAT I DECIDED at that time was not, as you may think, a break with Wagner – I felt a total aberration of my instincts of which the odd mistake, be it now Wagner or the chair at the University of Basel, was just another symptom. I became extremely *impatient* with myself; I realized that it was high time to reflect on *myself*. All at once I saw with terrible clarity how much time I had already wasted – how useless and arbitrary my whole existence as a philologist appeared in relation to my task. This false modesty embarrassed me… Ten years had passed in which the *nourishment* of my mind had truly ceased, in which I had learned nothing useful at all, in which I had forgotten absurd amounts for the sake of the rags and bones of learnedness. To crawl scrupulously with terrible eyesight through the metrics of Antiquity – that is what I had come to!

I looked at myself with overwhelming pity – how thin and emaciated I was: my learning simply lacked *realities* and my 'idealities' were not worth a damn! An almost all-consuming thirst took hold of me: from then on I really pursued nothing more than physiology, medicine and natural sciences – and I only returned to properly historical studies when the greater task compelled me to do so. It was then that I also realized for the first time the connection between an activity chosen against your better judgement, a so-called 'vocation' to which one is *barely* called, and that need for a dulling of the feeling of despondency and hunger by means of a narcotic art – for instance Wagnerian Art. As I carefully looked around me, I discovered that a large number of young men are in the same state of distress: one step against nature virtually *compels* another one. In German, in the 'German Empire' to speak unambiguously, all too many are condemned to choose vocations too early, and then to *waste away* under the heavy load, unable to shake it off. These people long for Wagner as a drug – they forget themselves, they lose themselves for a moment… what am I saying – *for five or six hours*!

4.

IT WAS THEN that my instinct decided inexorably against giving way, being a follower, being confused about myself. Any form of life, even the most unfavourable conditions like illness and poverty – they all seemed to me preferable to the unworthy 'selflessness' which I got mixed up with, originally because of ignorance and *youth*, and which I stuck to later because of inertia and a so-called 'sense of duty'. Here I was helped in a way that I cannot praise enough and just in time by my father's *malignant* heritage – basically a predestination to an early death. My illness *slowly set me free* – it spared me having to break away or take any violent or offensive step. I did not lose any goodwill then, but actually gained some. My illness also gave me the right to change all my habits completely; it allowed, even *commanded* me to forget; it granted me the necessity of lying still, of leisure, of waiting and being patient… But that means thinking!… My eyes themselves put an end to all that book-reading, in plain language: to philology. I was saved from the 'book', for years I did not read a thing – the *greatest* favour I ever did myself.

My most profound self, buried and silenced, as it were, by a constant barrage of *having* to listen to other selves (and that means reading!) woke up slowly, timidly, full of doubt – but at least *it was talking again*. Never have I been as happy as during the sickest and most painful periods of my life: just look at

Dawn or even *The Wanderer and His Shadow* to understand what this 'return to *myself*' meant: a supreme kind of *recovery*… The other kind, my cure, was merely a consequence of it.

5.

HUMAN, ALL TOO HUMAN, this monument to a rigorous self-discipline with which I abruptly ended all those effeminacies like 'supreme swindle', 'idealism', 'beautiful feelings' that had somehow wormed their way inside me, was for the most part written in Sorrento; I finished its final version during the winter months in Basel, under far less pleasant conditions than those in Sorrento. Actually, it is *Peter Gast*, a student at the University of Basel and very fond of me, who is responsible for this. I dictated it with my head bandaged, and in pain; he transcribed and corrected it – he was really the writer while I was merely the author. When the book was finally finished – to the amazement of the sick man – I also sent two copies to Bayreuth. By an extraordinary coincidence I received at the same time a beautiful copy of the *Parsifal* text dedicated to me by Richard Wagner with the inscription: 'To my dear friend Friedrich Nietzsche, from Richard Wagner, member of the Church Council'. To my ears, this crossing of the two books had an ominous ring. Did it not sound as if we had crossed *swords*?… Anyway, we both seemed to feel it, for we both remained silent.

Around that time the first *Bayreuth Blätter* appeared: I understood *what* I should have realized long ago – Incredible! Wagner had turned to religion…

6.

WHAT I THEN (1876) thought of myself, with what tremendous certainty I had my task and its world-historical aspect in my grasp, is testified by the book in general and by one passage in particular; only, once again with my inborn cunning I avoided the little word 'I' and showered with world-historical glory, this time not Schopenhauer or Wagner, but one of my friends, the excellent Dr Paul Rée – luckily far too sophisticated a creature to be deceived... *others* were less refined – I have always recognized the hopeless amongst my readers (for example, the typical German professor) by their reaction to this passage – they always had to see the whole book as a form of higher realism... In fact, the contents contradicted five or six propositions of my friend: you may wish to read the preface to my *On the Genealogy of Morals*.

The passage reads: 'But what is the main proposition at which one of the boldest and coldest thinkers has arrived, the author of the book *On the Origin of Moral Feelings* (read Nietzsche, the first immoralist) in virtue of his radical and penetrating analyses of human activity? "Moral man is no closer to the intelligible world than the physical man – since there is no intelligible world..."' This sentence, grown hard and sharp-edged under the hammer blow of historical recognition (read *Re-evaluation of all Values*) may perhaps one day, in some future (1890), serve as the axe aimed at the roots of the 'metaphysical needs' of humanity – but whether this is a blessing or a curse, who can say? However, it stands as a proposition of tremendous consequences, fruitful and dreadful at the same time and looking into the world possessed of that *double perspective* which all great insights share...

Dawn.
THOUGHTS ON MORALITY AS A PREJUDICE

1.

WITH THIS BOOK I begin my crusade against *morality*. Not that it smells in the least of gunpowder; you will notice very different, much lovelier scents, assuming that you have a reasonably sensitive nose. The guns are neither big nor small; if the effect of the book is negative, then its means are all the less so; these means that effect a conclusion, *not* a gunshot. To take leave in this book with a cautious reserve from all that was hitherto honoured and even worshipped under the name of morality in no way contradicts the fact that it contains not a single negative word, no attack, no spite – indeed, there it lies in the sunshine, well-rounded and happy, like some sea urchin basking in the sun among rocks. Ultimately, I myself was this sea urchin; almost each sentence of the book was first thought, was *hatched out* among that jumble of rocks near Genoa where I was alone and still in secret bond with the sea. Even now, whenever I touch that book by chance, almost every sentence becomes part of a net with which I can pull something unique back from the depths: its entire skin trembling with tender thrills of memory. The skill which distinguishes it is not least that it detains things for a little while, things that otherwise scurry past, weightlessly and noiselessly, moments I privately call divine lizards – not with the cruelty of that young Greek god who simply speared the poor little lizard, but all the same, I work with something pointed, with a pen... 'There are so many dawns that have not yet risen' – with this *Indian* inscription this book opens its doors. Where does its originator *seek* that new morning, that delicate red as yet undiscovered that will rise another day – what do I say, a whole series, a whole world of new days!? In a *re-evaluation of all values*, in liberation from all moral values, in saying 'Yes' and trusting all that has hitherto been forbidden, despised and cursed. This book, which says so firmly '*Yes*' pours out its light, its love, its tenderness for many wicked things; it gives them a 'soul', a 'good conscience', the lofty right and *privilege* of existence. Morality is not attacked, it is merely no longer in the picture... This book closes with 'don't you think?' – it is the only book that closes with 'don't you think?'...

2.

MY LIFE'S WORK lies in preparing humanity for a moment of intense self-examination, a *time of reckoning* when it will look backwards and outwards, then emerge from the dominion of chance and priests and for the first time ask itself the fundamental questions about 'Why?' and 'For What?' – this task is the necessary consequence of the knowledge that humanity is *not* capable of setting itself on the right path, that it is *not* in any way subject to divine rule; on the contrary, that actually precisely among their most holy regarded values the instinct for denial, the instinct for decadence, has been seductively in charge. The question concerning the origin of moral value is therefore for me a question of *the first order*, because it is crucial for the future of humanity. The demand that we should all *believe* ourselves basically in safe hands, that a book, the Bible, offers us a definitive assurance of divine governance and wisdom in the destiny of man, is translated back into reality, the will to suppress the truth about the pitiable opposite of all this, namely that so far humanity has been in the *worst* of hands and that it has been governed by the losers, two-faced vengeful ones, the so-called 'saints', these slanderers of the world and violators of men. The ultimate proof that the priest (and this includes the *clandestine* priest, the philosopher) is not just master of a certain religious community, but has become master in general, and that the morality of decadence, the will to the end, has been accepted as morality *itself*, is the fact that absolute value is afforded to all that is non-egoistic, and hostility to all that is egoistic. Those who do not agree with me at this point are in my opinion *infected*… But all the world disagrees with me… For a physiologist such a juxtaposition of values simply leaves no doubt. When even the least important organ within an organism fails to enforce its self-preservation, its restoration of energy, its 'egoism' with perfect certainty, then the whole will degenerate. The physiologist demands the degenerated part is *cut out*; he denies any solidarity with it, he has not the slightest pity for it.

However, it is precisely the *degeneration* of the whole, of humanity, that the priest *desires*; that is why he *conserves* what degenerates – that is his price for his governance… What is the point of those concepts of lies, the *ancillary* concepts of morality: 'soul', 'spirit', 'free will', 'God', if not to ruin humanity physiologically?… If you deflect seriousness from self-preservation, the build-up of physical strength, *that is of life*, if anaemia is construed as an ideal and contempt for the body as 'the salvation of the soul', what else is this if not a *recipe* for decadence? – The loss of the centre of gravity, the resistance to the natural instincts, in a word 'selflessness' – that is what until now was called *morality*… With *Dawn* I first took up the fight against the morality that would unself man.

THE JOYFUL SCIENCE.

DAWN is a positive book, profound but full of light and kindness. This is also true and to the highest degree of *The Joyful Science*; in almost every sentence, thoughtfulness and sense of mischief are lovingly combined in this book. A poem expressing thanks for the most wonderful January I ever lived through – the whole book is a gift – reveals most clearly from what sheer depth 'science' drew to become *joyful*…

> You, who with your spear aflame
> crushed the ice around my soul
> that rushing to the sea it came
> of its highest hope and goal:
> ever brighter, full of grace
> in its loving bond, but free –
> will it sing you songs of praise
> my beloved January.

Who can doubt what is meant here by 'highest hope' when at the close of the fourth book the crystalline beauty of the first words of *Zarathustra* rise in their shining glory? Or on reading the granite-like sentences at the end of the third book with which for the first time destiny is given a formula *for all time*? 'The Songs of Prince Outlaw', most of it was written in Sicily, remind us explicitly of the Provençal notion of *The Joyful Science*, that group of *singer, knight and free spirit* which distinguishes that wonderful early culture of Provence from all ambiguous cultures – in particular the last poem 'To the Mistral', an exuberant song in which, with respect, morality is freely trodden on, is perfectly typical for Provence.

THUS SPOKE ZARATHUSTRA.
A BOOK FOR ALL AND NO-ONE

1.

I SHALL NOW tell you the story of *Zarathustra*. The basic *idea* of the book, the notion of *eternal recurrence*, this highest formula of affirmation that could ever have been achieved, was conceived in August of 1881: it was drafted on a sheet of paper with the inscription: '6,000 feet beyond men and time'. I myself walked on that day from Lake Silvaplana through the forests; at a powerful pyramid-shaped boulder near Surlei I stopped to rest. There I had this thought: if I count back a few months from this day, I will discover, like an omen, a sudden and extremely decisive change in my taste, especially in music. You may of course altogether count *Zarathustra* as music – certainly a renaissance of the art of *listening* was a precondition for it. In a little mountain spa near Vicenza, Recoaro, where I spent the spring of 1881, I, together with my friend, the young musician Peter

Gast, another 'reborn' one, discovered that the phoenix of music flew past us with a lighter and more brilliant plumage than he had ever displayed before. But if I go forward from that day to the sudden birth under the most unlikely conditions in February 1883 (the final part, from which I quoted a few sentences in my *preface*, was finished in precisely that sacred hour in which Richard Wagner died in Venice), we arrive at eighteen months for the pregnancy. This figure of exactly eighteen months might suggest, at least to Buddhists, that I am really a female elephant.

The Joyful Science, its hundred indications showing that it is near to something quite incomparable, belongs to the interval period; in the end it even starts *Zarathustra* off, and it also delivers the fundamental concept of *Zarathustra* in the penultimate passage of the fourth book. Similarly, that 'Hymn to Life' (for mixed choir and orchestra) was composed during this interval; its score was published two years ago by EW Fritzsch in Leipzig. One symptom for my state of mind that year perhaps worth noting was the pure *positive* pathos that was particularly strong within me then; I called it the tragic pathos. The time will come when it will be sung in my memory. The text (I have to make this clear since this is currently often misunderstood) is not by me; it is the surprising inspiration of a young Russian woman who was my friend at that time, a Miss Lou von Salomé. If you can make any sense of the final words of this poem you will be able to imagine why I preferred and admired it – it has greatness. Pain is *not* held to be an objection to life: 'If you have no joy to give me, well then, *you still have your pain…*'

Perhaps my music, too, has some greatness when it comes to this passage (top note of the oboe, C sharp, not C: misprint). The following winter I stayed in that pretty quiet bay of Rapallo near Genoa, which is wedged between Chiavari and the foothills of Portofino. My health was not at its best back then: the winter was cold and excessively wet; a little hostel right next to the sea, so that the high waves made it impossible for me to sleep at night, was in just about every way the opposite of what I would have wished for. Nevertheless, and almost to prove my doctrine that anything of decision-making importance happens 'in spite of' and not 'because of', this winter and its inclement conditions saw my *Zarathustra* come into being.

In the morning I would climb upwards and southwards on the splendid road to Zoagli, right to the top, looking past pine trees to get a magnificent view of the sea. In the afternoon, whenever my health permitted it, I walked around the whole bay from Santa Margherita all the way to Portofino. This town and its landscape came even closer to my heart because of the great love which the unforgettable German Emperor Frederick III felt for them; by chance I was in this coastal region again in the autumn of 1886, when he visited this small forgotten world of happiness for a last time. It was on these two walks that Zarathustra first came to me, in particular as a type: indeed, he *overcame* me…

2.

TO UNDERSTAND this type we must first become familiar with his physiological condition: this is what I call *great health*. I cannot explain this concept better, more *personally* than I already did, that is to say in one of the final sections of the fifth book of *The Joyful Science*: 'Being new, nameless, incomprehensible, we premature births of an as yet unproven future need for a new goal also a new means – namely a new health, stronger, more seasoned, tougher, more audacious and more joyful than any previous one. Whoever has a soul that longs to have experienced the whole range of values and desires to date, and to have sailed around all the coast of this ideal "Mediterranean"; whoever wants to know from the adventures of his own more authentic experience how an explorer and conqueror of the ideal feels, and also an artist, a saint, a legislator, a sage, a scholar, a pious man, a soothsayer and a recluse of the old style – needs one thing above everything else: *great health* – a condition that we not merely have but also acquire continually. This condition we must acquire because it is relinquished again and again, and must be relinquished. And now, after having long been on our way in this manner, we Argonauts of the ideal, with more daring perhaps than is prudent, and having suffered shipwreck and damage often enough, but we are, to repeat it, healthier than they would like us to be, dangerously healthy, always regaining health – it will seem to us as if, as a reward, we have now confronted an as yet undiscovered country whose boundaries nobody has surveyed yet, something beyond all the lands and nooks of the ideal so far, a world so abundantly rich in beauty, strangeness, dubiousness, dreadfulness and heavenliness that our curiosity as well as our longing to possess it has got beside itself – oh, nothing will satisfy us now! After such sights and with such ravenous hunger for knowledge and conscience, how could we still be satisfied with *present-day man*? That is bad enough, but it is inevitable that we find it difficult to remain serious when we look at his worthiest goals and hopes, and perhaps we do not even bother to look any more.

'Another ideal runs ahead of us, an odd, tempting, dangerous ideal to which we should not wish to persuade anybody because we do not readily grant *the right to it* to anyone: the ideal of a spirit who plays naively – that is to say not deliberately but out of overflowing power and abundance – with all that was hitherto called holy, good, untouchable, divine; for whom those supreme things which the people naturally accept as the measure of their values, signify danger, decay, humiliation, or at least recreation, blindness, and temporary self-oblivion; the ideal of a human-superhuman well-being and benevolence that will often appear *inhuman* (for example, when it confronts all previous earthly seriousness, all previous solemnity in gesture, word, tone, eye, morality, and sense of duty, as if it were their most lifelike and unintended parody) and with which in spite of all of this perhaps *great seriousness* will really begin, the real question mark will be set for the first time, the destiny of the soul will take a turn, the hand of the clock will move on, the tragedy will *take its course…*'

3.

HAS ANYONE at the end of the 19th century a clear idea of what poets of strong ages called *inspiration*? If not, I shall describe it. If you had the least remains of superstition in you, you could indeed hardly reject the idea you are merely the plaything and mouthpiece of, and medium for, overpowering forces. The concept of revelation in the sense that suddenly with incredible certainty and subtlety something becomes *visible*, audible, something that shakes you to the core and takes you over, merely describes the facts. You listen out, you do not seek; you take, you do not ask who gives; like lightning a thought flashes up, urging, unfaltering – I never had a choice. It is a rapture – its tremendous tension may occasionally find relief in floods of tears, now the pace quickens unintentionally, now it slows down; a complete frenzy while being distinctly aware of countless subtle thrills that make your skin tingle right down to your toes; a depth of happiness in which the most poignant and most dismal do not seem to be at odds, but rather a condition, challenged, a *much-needed* splash of colour within such an excess of light; an instinct for rhythmic relationships reaching across wide spaces – length, the need for *all-embracing* rhythm is almost the measure of the force of inspiration, a kind of counterpoint to its pressure and tension...

Everything happens completely involuntarily but as in a gale of yearning for freedom, of absoluteness, of power, of divinity... The randomness of image and simile is strangest of all; there is no longer a notion of what is an image or a simile, everything offers itself as the nearest, the most obvious, the simplest expression. It really seems, to bring something that Zarathustra said to mind, as if the things came by themselves and offered themselves as similes ('here come all things with caresses to your discourse and flatter you: for they want to ride on your back. On every simile you ride to every truth. Here the words and receptacles of words all burst open for you; all being wishes to become word, all becoming wishes to learn from you how to speak'). This is *my* experience of inspiration; I do not doubt that you have to go back thousands of years to find anyone who could tell me, 'It is mine too'.

4.

AFTERWARDS I was ill for a few weeks in Genoa. Then there followed a melancholy spring in Rome where I put up with life – it was not easy. Basically, I was hugely irritated by this location, the most unsuitable location in the world for the poet of *Zarathustra*, where I was not by choice. I tried to get away – I wanted to go to *Aquila*, precisely the opposite of Rome, founded as an act of hostility to Rome, as I shall one day found a place in memory of an atheist and enemy of the church of the first order, one of those closest related to me, the great Emperor Frederick II of the Hohenstaufen dynasty. But somehow I could not escape the capital: I had to go back again. In the end, after I had given up trying to find an *anti-Christian* region, I resigned myself to the Piazza Barberini. I fear that in order to avoid bad smells as much as possible, I even asked in the residence of the King of Italy itself whether they did not have a quiet room for a philosopher.

On a loggia high above that Piazza, from which you have a view over all of Rome and can listen to the fountain running deep below, I composed that loneliest of lonely songs that has ever been written, 'The Night Song'; at that time a melody of inexpressible melancholy was always in my head and I used the words 'death from immortality' in the chorus…

That summer, back home at the sacred spot where the first lightning flash of *Zarathustra* had dazzled me, I found *Zarathustra II*. I only needed ten days: I never needed any more time, for the first or for the third and the final section either. In the following winter under the peaceful sky of Nice that sparkled above me for the first time in my life, I found *Zarathustra III* – and was finished; scarcely a year was all it took. Many hidden places and heights in the landscape around Nice are made very special for me by unforgettable moments; that decisive passage titled 'On Old and New Tablets' was composed during the difficult climb from the station to the marvellous Moorish aerie, Eza – I was always fittest when on top of my creative force. The *body* is inspired; let us keep the 'soul' out of it... I was often seen to dance; in those days I could walk in the mountains for seven, eight hours without feeling in the least bit tired. I slept well, I laughed much – I was at the height of my vigour and patience.

5.

APART FROM these ten-day oeuvres, the years during and in particular *after* my *Zarathustra* were a calamity beyond comparison. You pay dearly to be immortal: you have to die several times during your lifetime.

There is something that I would call the grudge of greatness: everything that is great, a work, a deed, will turn, once completed, *against* the one who accomplished it, and precisely because he accomplished it, he has become *weak* – he cannot bear his deed any longer, he can no longer face it. To have put something *behind* you that you were never permitted to choose, something into which the destiny of mankind has been knotted – and now you labour *under* it!... It almost crushes you. The grudge of Greatness! Then there is the eerie silence around you. Loneliness has seven skins – nothing can penetrate it. You meet people, greet friends: new bleakness, no-one looks you in the eye. At best this is a form of rebellion. I experienced such a rebellion; it was of a different nature but from almost everyone close to me: it seems that nothing is more insulting than to create a sudden distance – those *noble* natures who cannot live without worshipping someone are rare. Thirdly, there is the absurd sensitivity of the skin to small barbs, a kind of helplessness before everything petty. This seems to me due to an enormous squandering of all defensive energies, which are a condition for every *creative* deed, every deed that stems from our most authentic, inmost, nethermost regions. The *limited* abilities to defend yourself are thereby as good as suspended; no energy goes back into them. Moreover, I dare to suggest that our digestive system is hampered, we are less keen to move, that we are all too susceptible to chills as well as mistrust – mistrust which in many cases is merely an error caused by illness. In such a condition I once sensed the close presence of a herd of cows even before I set eyes on them, because milder, more philanthropic thoughts came back to me: *they* had warmth…

6.

THIS WORK stands very much on its own. Let us leave the poets out of it, perhaps nothing has ever been done from such an abundance of energy. My concept of the 'Dionysian' became a *supreme deed* here; all human action up to now seems poor and relative in comparison. The least we can say is that a Goethe, a Shakespeare would be unable to breathe even for a moment at this incredible height of passion, that Dante is merely a believer compared with Zarathustra and not one who first *creates* truth, a *world-governing* spirit and destiny – that the poets of the Vedic texts are priests and not even worthy of tying the shoelaces of Zarathustra and it does not give the slightest idea of the distance, of the *mountain blue* solitude in which this work dwells. Zarathustra has for ever a right to say, 'I draw circles around me and sacred boundaries; fewer and fewer climb with me on ever higher mountains – I build a mountain range out of ever more sacred mountains.' Add up the spirit and goodness of all great souls: all of them together would not be able to speak like Zarathustra. The scale on which he ascends and descends is tremendous; he has seen further, strives to go further, *could* go further than any other human being. He contradicts with his every word, this most positive of all minds; in him all opposites are blended into a new unity. The highest and the lowest energies of human nature, the sweetest, airiest and most dreadful ones surge forth from a well with immortal certainty. Until then, you do not know what height is, what depth is, you know even less what truth is. There is not a moment in this revelation of truth that has already been anticipated or conjectured by one of the greatest. Before Zarathustra, there was no wisdom, no soul searching, no art of oratory; even everyday matters, the most humdrum, speak of extraordinary things. Aphorisms are trembling with passion; eloquence becomes music; lightning bolts are hurled into hitherto unfathomed futures. The most powerful capacity for simile that has existed so far is poor and a mere toy compared with this return of language to the nature of symbolism.

Look, how Zarathustra descends and says something kind to everyone! How gently his hands touch even his antagonists, the priests, and how he suffers *with* them. Here, man is overcome every moment that passes, the concept of 'Superman' has here become the greatest reality – whatever has been great in man up to now lies *beneath* him at an infinite distance. The peaceful, the light-footed, the omnipresence of wickedness and high spirits and all other things typical of the type of Zarathustra, has never been dreamed of as being essential to greatness. Precisely in this immense space with its access to the contradictory, Zarathustra feels himself to be *the supreme type of all beings*; and if you hear his definition of it, you will not bother trying to look for a simile for him.

'– the soul which has the longest ladder and can go down the deepest,

the most comprehensive soul which can walk and go astray and roam furthest within itself,

the one most necessary, which flings itself with joyful passion into chance,

the soul as being, which *will* strive to become, the one as having, which *will* strive to want and desire,

the one in flight from itself, closing in on itself in the widest possible circle,

the wisest soul, enticed most sweetly by folly,

the one that loves itself the most, in which all matters have their currents and counter-currents, their low and high tides.'

But that is the concept of Dionysus himself. Another contemplation led us to precisely this point. The psychological problem with the type of Zarathustra is, how he who says 'No' and *does* 'No' to everything to which we have until now said 'Yes' to an unheard-of degree, can nevertheless be the opposite of a No-saying spirit; how the spirit bearing the most terrible fate, a doomed task, can nevertheless be the lightest and the most ethereal – Zarathustra is a dancer. How he who has the hardest, the most dreadful insight into reality, who thought the 'most abysmal thought' nevertheless does not consider it an objection to existence, not even to its eternal recurrence – but rather one reason more for *being himself* the eternal 'Yes' to all things, 'the tremendous, boundless saying of "Yes" and "Amen"'... 'Into all abysses I still carry the blessings of my "Yes"'... *But that is the concept of Dionysus once again.*

7.

WHAT LANGUAGE will such a spirit speak when he speaks to himself? The language of the *dithyramb*, the song of praise to Dionysus. I am the inventor of the dithyramb. Listen all to how Zarathustra talks to himself before *sunrise* (III, 18): such emerald happiness, such divine tenderness had no tongue before me. Even the profoundest sadness of such a Dionysus still becomes a song of his praise; take for instance 'The Night Song' – the immortal lament at being condemned by the abundance of light and power, by his *sun* nature, not to love.

'It is night: now all fountains speak louder. And my soul too is a fountain.

It is night: only now all songs of lovers are roused. And my soul too is the song of a lover.

Something not stilled, which cannot be stilled is within me that wants to raise its voice. A desire for love is within me that itself speaks the language of love.

I am light: ah, that I were night! But this is my loneliness: I am girded by light.

Ah, that I were dark and of the night! How I would suck at the breasts of light!

And I would even bless you yourselves, you little twinkling stars and glow-worms up there! – and be overjoyed because of your gifts of light.

But I live in my own light, I drink the flames that break out of me back into myself.

I do not know the happiness of those who take, and I have often dreamed that stealing must be still more blissful than taking.

This is my poverty that my hand never rests from giving; that is my envy that I see waiting eyes and the illuminated nights of longing.

Oh misery of all givers; eclipse of my sun; craving to crave; ravenous hunger while filling up!

They take from me: but do I still touch their soul? There is a chasm between taking and giving, and the smallest chasm is the last to be bridged.

Hunger grows out of my beauty: I should like to hurt those for whom I light the way, I should like to rob those to whom I gave – thus I hunger for wickedness.

Withdrawing my hand just as the other hand reaches out

to it, like a waterfall that hesitates even as it plunges: this is how I hunger for wickedness.

Such revenge is plotted by my abundance, such spite wells up out of my loneliness.

My happiness in giving died while giving; my virtue became weary of itself in its abundance.

Those who always give are in danger of losing their shame; those who always hand out grow callouses on heart and hand from all that handing out.

My eye no longer sheds tears because of the shame of those asking; my hand has become too hard for the trembling of filled hands.

Where have the tears in my eyes gone and the downiness of my heart? Oh the loneliness of all givers, the silence of all who shine!

Many suns circle in barren space: to all that is dark they speak with their light – to me they do not speak.

This is the hostility of the light towards those who shine: merciless, it travels in its orbit.

Unjust to those who shine in its innermost heart, cold towards suns – thus travels every sun.

The suns travel like a storm in their orbits; they follow their implacable will – that is their coldness. Oh it is only you, you dark ones, you of the night, who create warmth from that which shines! Only you drink milk and refreshment from the udders of light.

Ah, ice is around me, my hand is burned by iciness; thirst is within me, which pines for your thirst.

It is night: ah, that I must be light! And thirst for things of the night! And loneliness!

It is night: now my longing breaks out of me like a well – I long for speech.

It is night: now all fountains talk louder. And my soul too is a fountain.

It is night: now all songs of lovers are roused. And my soul too is the song of a lover.'

8.

NOTHING LIKE THIS has ever been written, ever been felt or *suffered*: this is how a god, a Dionysus, suffers. The answer to such a song of solar solitude in the light would be Ariadne… Who apart from me knows what Ariadne is!… No one so far knows the solution of such riddles, I doubt that anyone ever even saw it as riddle. Zarathustra defines once, with rigour, his task – it is mine too – so that we cannot be mistaken as to the *meaning*; he *says 'Yes'* to the point of justification, to the point of redemption of all things past too.

'I travel amongst men as amongst fragments of the future: the future which I envisage.

And that is all my poetry and striving, that I can write poetry and gather all at once what is fragment and riddle and dreadful chance.

And how could I bear to be human if man was not also a poet, and solver of riddles and redeemer of the future?

To redeem those from the past and to turn every "it was" into a "that is how I wanted it": that alone I should call redemption.'

In another passage he defines as rigorously as possible what for him alone 'man' can be – *not* an object of love or, worse, compassion – Zarathustra even mastered the *great disgust* for man: man to him is a shapeless thing, a material, an ugly stone that needs a sculptor.

'No longer to *want* and no longer to *appreciate* and no longer to *create*: oh that this great weariness might always remain far from me!

In knowledge too I only feel my will's joy in begetting and becoming and if there is innocence in my knowledge, it is because the *will to beget* is part of it.

This will has lured me away from God and the gods: what is there to create if gods – were there?

But my fervent will to create drives me again and again towards man; thus is the hammer driven to the stone.

Ah, you men, within the stone sleeps an image for me to see, the image of all images! Ah, that it must sleep in the hardest, ugliest stone.

Now my hammer rages brutally against its prison. Pieces of rock rain from the stone: what is that to me!

I want to perfect it, for a shadow came to me – once, the quietest and lightest of all things came to me!

The beauty of superman came to me as a shadow: what are the gods to me now!…'

I wish to stress a final point: the line in italics demands it. Among the conditions for a Dionysian task is most certainly the hardness of the hammer, *the joy even in destroying*. The imperative 'Harden!', the certainty deep below *that all creators are hard* is the distinctive mark of a Dionysian nature.

BEYOND GOOD AND EVIL
PROLOGUE TO A PHILOSOPHY OF THE FUTURE

1.

MY TASK for the following years has been as strictly sketched out as is possible. Now that the Yes-saying part has been achieved, it is the turn of the No-saying, *No*-doing part, the re-evaluation of the previous values themselves, the great war – the evocation of a day for the big decision. This includes the slow turning round to look for my peers, to those strong enough to offer me their help *destroying*.

From then on, all my writings are fishhooks: perhaps I am as good an angler as anyone else?... If I caught nothing, it's not my fault. *There just weren't any fish...*

2.

IN ALL THAT MATTERS, this book (1886) is a *critique of modernity*, including modern science, modern art, even modern politics, whilst pointing to an antagonistic type that has very little in common with modern man: a noble, Yes-saying type. In this latter sense, the book is a *school for gentlemen*, the term here being used in a more spiritual and radical sense than ever before. You have to have inbuilt courage to put up with it and never have known fear... All those things on which this era prides itself are seen as conflicting with this type, making them almost seem like bad manners: the famous 'objectivity' for instance, the 'compassion with all suffering', the 'historical sense' with its slavish devotion to all things foreign, subservience to inferior notions and 'all concepts of science'. If you keep in mind that the book was written *after Zarathustra*, you may be able to imagine where it comes from. The eye, compelled by a tremendous urge to look out into the *far* distance (and Zarathustra is even more farsighted than the Tsar) is here forced to focus sharply on what is close at hand: our own age and *environment*. You will find in every detail and in particular in outline a *deliberate* renunciation of those instincts which made a *Zarathustra* possible. Refinement of form, intention and the *art of being silent* are emphasized; psychology is handled with deliberate hardness and cruelty – the book has not a single kind word…

All that is restful: who can conceive in the end *which* type of rest makes such a waste of goodness necessary as is found in *Zarathustra*?… Theologically speaking – listen well, because I seldom speak as a theologian – it was God Himself who, at the end of His day's work, coiled Himself up as a snake beneath the tree of knowledge: that was His way of resting from His task of being God… He had made everything too beautiful. The devil is simply God's idleness on every seventh day.

THE GENEALOGY OF MORALS.
A POLEMICAL PAPER

THE THREE TREATISES which make up this genealogy are, as regards expression, intention and technique of the unexpected, perhaps the most sinister that have ever been written. Dionysus, as we know, is also the god of darkness. This is a starting line that is *calculated* to lead you astray every time – cool, scientific, even ironical, deliberately pushy and deliberately reticent. Gradually the atmosphere becomes restless, there is the odd flash of lightning, very uncomfortable truths make themselves heard from afar with a dull rumbling sound – until finally with ferocious speed the moment comes where all is driven forward with terrible intensity. And at the last, amongst dreadful detonations, a *new* truth peeps at you through thick clouds.

The truth of the *first* treatise is the psychology of Christianity: the birth of Christianity out of the spirit of resentment, not, as may have been believed, out of 'spirit' – it is a countermovement in its nature, the grand uprising against domination by *noble* values. The *second* treatise deals with the psychology of *conscience*: this is *not*, as may well have been believed, 'the voice of God in man', but the instinct of cruelty turning in on itself after it can no longer release itself to the outside world. Cruelty is here revealed, for the first time, as one of the oldest and most indispensable elements of culture. The *third* treatise is a reply to the question as to the origin of the tremendous power of the ascetic ideal, the priest ideal, even though it is a *harmful* ideal in every sense, the will to annihilation and an ideal of decadence. This is the reply: it is powerful *not* because God's presence is behind the priest, which may well have been believed, but for lack of something better and because so far it has been the only ideal – after all, it has no competition. 'For man would rather aspire to nothingness than *not* aspire at all'… Above all, *apart from* Zarathustra there was no *counter-ideal*.

You get my meaning. Three decisive psychological

overtures for a re-evaluation of all values. This book contains the first psychology of the priest.

THE TWILIGHT OF THE IDOLS.
HOW TO PHILOSOPHIZE WITH A SLEDGEHAMMER

1.

THIS BOOK of less than 150 pages, both cheerful and fatalistic in its tone (a demon laughing at you, so to speak, and the work of so few days that I cannot even be bothered to tell you how many) is altogether an exception amongst books: there is no book richer in substance, more independent, more dazzling – more wicked! If you wish to get an idea of how everything stood on its head in front of me, start by reading this work. What is called '*idol*' in the title is simply everything that hitherto has been called truth. *The Twilight of the Idols* – in plain language: the old truth is coming to an end...

2.

THERE IS NO REALITY, no 'notion of an ideal' that has not been touched upon in this book (touched! what cautious euphemism!). Not just the *eternal* idols, but also the very recent and therefore most senile ones: 'Modern ideas' for instance. A powerful wind blows between the trees and everywhere fruit – truths – drops down. It smacks of the windfall of an autumn all too fruitful: you trip over truths, you even crush some to death – there are just too many...

However, what you can grasp is no longer questionable, these are decisions. I alone hold the yardstick for 'truths' in my hands, I alone *can* decide. It is as if a *second* consciousness had grown within me, as if my 'will' had cast a light upon the *downward* slope along which it has been running for ages... The *downward* slope – they called it the road to the 'truth'... All 'dark urges' have been dealt with, indeed, the *good* human being was least aware of the righteous path.

And in all seriousness, nobody before me knew of the righteous path, the path leading upwards: I alone pointed towards hopes, tasks and recommended paths of culture – *I am the herald of these good tidings...* And therefore I am also destiny.

3.

IMMEDIATELY after finishing this work and without losing a single day, I took upon myself the formidable task of the *re-evaluation* with a supreme feeling of pride which nothing could equal. Aware of my immortality at every moment, I engraved sign after sign into brass tablets with the certainty of fate. The preface was written on 3rd September 1888. When, after finishing it, I stepped outside into the morning air, I found the most lovely day I have ever lived through in the Upper Engadine – clear, glowing in its colours and with all its contrasts, all hues available between the icy north and the south.

Owing to a delay caused by floods, I did not leave Sils-Maria until 20th September, so in the end I was the only visitor in this delectable spot, which in my gratitude I wish to make immortal. After an eventful journey, including one narrow escape from death in the waters of Lake Como, which was flooded when I reached it in the dead of night, I arrived in Turin, to which I was *guided*, on the afternoon of the 21st, and it was from that time on my home.

I took the same lodgings I had occupied in the spring, on Via Carlo Alberto 6, III, opposite the mighty Palazzo Carignano where Vittorio Emanuele was born; it has a view of the Piazza Carlo Alberto and to the hills beyond it. Without hesitating and without being swayed for one moment, I returned to my work: only the last quarter of the book still remained to be written. The 30th September, Victory!, was the seventh day and a God could take it easy, walking along the River Po. The same day, I wrote the preface for my *Twilight of the Idols* for which I had corrected the proofs at leisure during the month of September.

Never before have I lived through an autumn like that, nor even imagined that such glory could be possible – a Claude Lorrain painting extended to infinity, every day of an equally incredible perfection.

THE WAGNER CASE
A MUSICIAN'S PROBLEM.

1.

TO DO THIS ESSAY JUSTICE you have to suffer from the fatal affliction of music as from an open wound. *From what* do I suffer, when I suffer from the fatal affliction of music? I suffer because music has been deprived of its transfiguring, positive character – because it has become the music of decadence and is no longer the flute of Dionysus…

Supposing, however, that you feel that the cause of music is very much your *own* cause, your *own* tale of woe, then you will find this essay considerate and extremely mild in tone. To be cheerful in such cases and self-deprecating in a good-humoured way, in other words, to speak the truth whilst laughing whereby the truth would justify the hardest language, that is humanitarianism itself. Who would seriously doubt that I, old war horse that I am, will bring out my big guns against Wagner? – I restrained myself from any decisive action in this cause – I loved Wagner!

In the end this is an attack on a more subtle 'unknown figure' who cannot be easily divined by anyone in the sense that I wish to insinuate (really! I have to expose 'unknown figures' of a very different calibre to some adventurer in music). However, it is even more so an attack on the German nation, whose mind is becoming lazier and less instinctive but ever more *honest* and continues to feed itself with an enviable appetite on polarities, gulping 'faith', as well as scholarship, 'Christian love', as well as anti-Semitism, the will to power (the 'Empire') as well as the Gospel of the Humble without any sign of indigestion… This lack of judgement in choosing between these opposites! This ventral neutrality and 'selflessness'. This fairness of the German *taste bud* that will level everything – that finds everything tasty… Without any doubt, the Germans are idealists! When I last visited Germany, I found German taste occupied with trying to put Wagner and the Trumpeter of Säckingen on the same level; I myself was witness as the citizens of Leipzig founded a Liszt society in honour of one of the most genuine and German musicians (in the old sense of the term German, not an 'imperial' German), Master *Heinrich Schütz*, in order to foster and spread '*listed* church music'… Without any doubt, Germans are idealists!

2.

BUT NOTHING shall stop me from becoming rude and telling the Germans a few hard truths: *who else will do it*? I speak of their historical perversion. Not only have German historians lost altogether the *grand view* for the course and values of culture and have, to a man, become buffoons of politics (or the church): they have even *outlawed* this grand view. First and foremost you have to be 'German', of 'good race', then you may settle all historical values and non-values by arbitration.

'German' is an argument; 'Germany, Germany above all' is a principle; the Germans represent the 'moral world order' in history. In relation to the Roman Empire they are the bringers of freedom, in relation to the 18th century they are the restorers of morality, of the 'categorical imperative'… There is an imperial German historiography, even, I fear, an anti-Semitic one, a *court* historiography, and Mr von Treitschke does not seem to be embarrassed by it…

The other day, an idiotic judgement of *history*, a proposition by the (fortunately) deceased Swabian aesthetician Vischer went the rounds of the German newspapers as a 'truth' that every German had to *accept*: 'The Renaissance *and* the Reformation – both together they constitute a whole – the aesthetic rebirth *and* the moral rebirth'. Such announcements make me lose my patience and I feel inclined, even duty bound, to tell the Germans once and for all *what* else they have already on their conscience. *Every great cultural crime for four centuries is what they have on their conscience!*... And always from the same cause – from their innermost *cowardice* in the face of reality, which has become cowardice in the face of truth, from their now instinctive lack of truthfulness, from 'idealism'... The Germans have cheated Europe of the harvest, of the meaning of the last *great* era – the Renaissance – at a moment when a higher order of values, noble, life- and future-affirming values had been victorious at the seat of anti-ethical values, the *values of decline – and entered deeply into the instincts of those that dwelled there.* Luther, this calamity of a monk, restored the church and, much, much worse, Christianity, at the moment *of its fall...* Christianity, this *negation of the will to live* that became a religion! Luther, an impossible monk who precisely because of his 'impossibleness' attacked the church and thus – as a consequence – restored it. The Catholics would have good reason to celebrate Luther Festivals, to compose Luther plays! Luther... and the 'moral rebirth'! To hell with all psychology! Without doubt, the Germans are idealists.

Twice before, when incredible courage and willpower just managed to attain a decent, an unambiguous, a completely scientific mode of thinking, the Germans have known how to find rat runs back to the old 'ideal', to reconciliations between truth and 'ideal', at bottom formulas for the right to reject science, for the right to *lie*: in the form of Leibniz and Kant – these two largest stumbling blocks of Europe's intellectual integrity. Finally, when on the cusp between two decadent centuries a sweeping force of genius and will made itself known, strong enough to unite Europe, a political and *economic* union for the purpose of global government, the Germans with their 'Wars of Liberation' cheated Europe of the meaning, the miracle of meaning in the person of Napoleon – they thereby have on their conscience all that followed, all that we see today, this sickness and lack of reason *inimical to culture* – nationalism – this national neurosis which Europe suffers from, reinforcing Europe's system of mini-states, of *petty* politics: they have made Europe lose its mind, its reason – they have led it into a blind alley. Does anyone apart from me know a way out of this blind alley?… A task, *great* enough to *unite* people once again?

3.

AND LAST but not least, why should I not voice my suspicion? In my case too, the Germans will try once again everything to breed a mouse from a tremendous destiny. So far, they have shown themselves up for what they are with regards to me; I doubt that they will do any better in the future. What I wouldn't give to be wrong here, to be a *bad* prophet!…

My natural readers and listeners even now are Russians, Scandinavians and the French – will this always be the case? The Germans have entered nothing but ambiguous names into the history of the quest for knowledge; they have only ever produced 'unconscious' frauds (this befits Fichte, Schelling, Schopenhauer, Hegel, Schleiermacher as well as it does Kant and Leibniz – they are all only pulling the wool over our eyes); they shall never be privileged to be counted as one with the first spirit of *integrity* in the history of the spirit, the spirit which does justice to the truth of fraudulence of four thousand years. The 'German spirit' seems stuffy to me: I breathe with difficulty near this psychological squalor that has become instinctive and is revealed by every word and in every countenance of a German. They have never lived through a 17th century of tough self-examination like the French – a La Rochefoucauld, a Descartes, are a hundred times superior to the best German in integrity – to this day they have not had a psychologist. But psychology is almost a yardstick for the *cleanliness* or *squalor* of a race... And if you are not even clean, how can you have *depth*? You will never get to the bottom of it with a German, almost as with women, *there is none*, that is all there is to it. They are not even shallow. What is called 'deep' in Germany is precisely this instinctive squalor turned against themselves of which I have just spoken: they *do not want* to see themselves clearly. Might I suggest to use the word 'German' as an international coinage for this psychological depravity?

For example, at this very moment the German Emperor calls it his 'Christian duty' to free the slaves in Africa: we other Europeans would then simply be calling this 'German'... Have the Germans produced even a single book of any depth? They do not even have a notion of depth in a book. I have met scholars who thought of Kant as deep; I am afraid that at the Prussian court, Mr von Treitschke is considered deep. And on occasions when I praised Stendhal as a deep psychologist, I have met German university professors who asked me how to spell his name...

4.

AND WHY should I not go all the way? I like to make a clean sweep of things. I even have the ambition of appearing to be the supreme rejecter of Germans. Even at twenty-six I expressed my mistrust of the German character (Third Untimely Meditation, section 6) – I can't stand the Germans. If I had to invent a type of person who antagonizes all my instincts, he would always turn into a German.

The acid test for me is whether a man can see things as they are, whether he recognizes rank, degree or the hierarchy which is natural to people, whether he *distinguishes*: if so, he is a gentleman; otherwise he belongs hopelessly to the broadminded, oh such good-natured category of the scoundrel. But that is what the Germans are – scoundrels – oh, they are so very good-natured… You debase yourself when associating with Germans: the Germans make everyone *look equal*.

Not counting my association with a few artists, in particular with Richard Wagner, I have not spent one good hour with a German… If the most profound spirit of all time were to appear among Germans, some silly goose would believe that her not-so-beautiful soul deserved at least as much attention… I can't bear this race which is always bad company, has no feelings for nuances (oh dear! I am a nuance), has no life in its feet and cannot even walk… Ultimately, the Germans have no feet at all, just legs… They have no idea how common they are, but this is the superlative of vulgarity – they are not even *ashamed* of being merely Germans… They have to join in every conversation, they think of themselves as decision-makers, I am afraid that they have reached a decision even with regards to me…

My whole life is essentially the proof for all this. In vain do I look for some sign of tact, of sensitivity in their treatment of me. From Jews, yes, but never ever from a German. My nature demands that I am kind and gentle towards everyone – it is my *right*, not to differentiate – however, that does not stop me keeping my eyes open. I do not exclude anyone, least of all my friends – in the end I hope that this has not diminished my humanity towards them. There are five or six things which have always been a point of honour with me.

Nevertheless it remains true that almost every letter that has reached me for some years now strikes me as a piece of cynicism: there is more cynicism in goodwill for me than in any hatred... I tell every one of my friends to his face that he has never thought it worthwhile to *study* any of my books; I take it from the smallest sign that they don't even know what they are about. As for my Zarathustra, who of my friends would have seen more in him than a forbidden, fortunately perfectly meaningless presumption?...

Ten years, and nobody in Germany took it upon himself to defend my name against the absurd silence under which it was buried: it was a foreigner, a Dane, who was the first to have sufficient refinement of instinct and enough courage to take up arms against my so-called friends... Which German university these days would offer lectures on my philosophy as did Dr Georg Brandes in Copenhagen, who therewith once more proved himself a true psychologist?

As it is, I myself never suffered on account of all this; *necessaries* do not hurt me – love of destiny is my inmost nature. However, that does not preclude my love of irony, even world-historical irony. And thus, approximately two years before the shattering lightning bolt of *re-evaluation* which will convulse the earth, I have sent *The Wagner Case* into the world: let the Germans one more time assault me and this time *once and for all*! There is just about enough time left!

Has it been achieved? I am delighted, my dear Teutonic gentlemen, I must pay you my compliments... Just now, lest my friends be left out, one of my old girlfriends wrote to me that she now laughs at me... And this at a moment when an indescribable responsibility weighs on me – when no word can be too carefully chosen, no-one can look with sufficient awe at me. For I carry the destiny of mankind on my shoulders...

Chapter 4
Why I am destiny

1.

I KNOW MY FATE. One day, my name will be associated with the memory of something tremendous – a crisis without equal on earth, the most profound collision of conscience, a decision that was conjured up *against* everything that mankind has ever believed in and held sacred. I am no man, I am dynamite.

Yet for all that I am not a founder of a religion – religions are for the rabble. Whenever I come into contact with a religious person, I have to wash my hands afterwards. I don't *want* 'believers'; I think I am too wicked to believe in myself; I never address crowds... I am terribly afraid that one day I will be *canonized*: they will work out why I published this book *beforehand*, it is to prevent being taken the wrong way... I do not want to be a saint, I would sooner be a buffoon... Perhaps I am a buffoon... And yet or perhaps not yet (for there is nothing more false than a saint), the truth speaks out of me. But my truth is *terrible*: for until now they have called *lies* the truth. *Re-evaluation of all Values*: that is my formula for an act of supreme self-examination of mankind that became my flesh and my genius. It is my fate that I have to be the first *decent* person, that I find myself opposing the falsehood of thousands of years...

I was the first to *discover* the truth by being the first to find out that a lie is a lie – I could smell it... My genius lies in my nostrils... I dispute in a way that has never been done before and yet I am the opposite of a negative spirit. I am the bringer of glad tidings like no-one before me; I know tasks so enormous that hitherto no term could do justice to them, I alone will offer hope once again. For all that, I am necessarily also a man of destiny. For when truth declares war on the lies of thousands of years, we shall have upheavals, a convulsion of earthquakes, a moving of mountains and valleys the like of which has never been dreamed of. The concept of politics will have merged entirely with a war of ghosts, all power structures of the old society will have been blown to bits – all of them are founded on lies: there will be wars the like of which have never been seen on earth. I alone am responsible for *great politics* on earth.

2.

DO YOU WANT a formula for a destiny such that becomes *Son of Man*? – You will find it in my *Zarathustra*.

'*– and whoever wants to become a creator in good or evil, must first be a destroyer and dismantle values.*

Therefore the greatest evil is part of the greatest goodness: but this is being creative.'

I am by far the most awful human being that ever lived. However, that does not mean I will not also be the kindest. I know the pleasure in *destroying* to a degree that is in line with my strength to destroy – in both respects I obey my Dionysian nature which does not know how to separate doing 'No' from saying 'Yes'. I am the first *immoralist* – that makes me the perfect *destroyer*.

3.

NO-ONE ASKED ME but they should have asked me what the name of Zarathustra means when I speak it, I, the first immoralist: for the tremendous uniqueness of that historical Persian lies precisely in his contradictions. Zarathustra first saw the true wheel of fate in the fight with good and evil – the transmission of morality into metaphysics, as a force, a cause, a purpose in itself – that is *his* work. But this question is at heart already the reply. Zarathustra *created* this most fatal mistake – morality – therefore he also had to be the first to *recognize* it. Not just because he has more experience than any other thinker in this field, after all the whole history is the experimental dispute of the doctrine of the so-called 'ethical world order'; no, it is more important to say that Zarathustra is more truthful than any other thinker. His teaching and his teaching alone recognizes truth as the highest virtue; it means, it is the opposite of the *cowardice* of the 'idealist', who runs away from reality. Zarathustra is more courageous than all other thinkers put together and he *is able to shoot with arrow and bow* – that is the Persian virtue. Do you get my meaning?… Self-conquest of morality has its roots in truth, the self-conquest of the moralist in his opposite – in *me* – that is to say, when I speak the name of Zarathustra.

4.

BASICALLY there are two negations in my definition of *immoralist*: firstly, I deny a type of man that has so far been considered the very best, the *good*, the *complaisant*, the *charitable*; and then I negate a type of morality which became prevalent and predominant as morality itself – the morality of decadence or, to put it more plainly, *Christian* morality. It would be permissible to see the second objection as the more important one, since the overrating of goodness and kindness on a large scale is to my mind already the consequence of decadence, a symptom of weakness, incompatible with the force-gathering and positive life: negating and *destroying* are conditions of saying 'Yes'.

For now, I shall stick to the psychology of the good person. To estimate how much an archetypal person is worth, you have to calculate the price that his keep will cost – you have to know the conditions he needs for his existence. The condition for the existence of the good is the *lie* – put differently, not *wanting* to look reality in the face at any cost, in particular *not* in such a way as to ever challenge complaisant instincts, and even less in such a way as to put up with the interference of short-sightedly good-natured ones. To consider any *difficulties* in general as an objection, as something that has to be abolished, is absolute nonsense, and on a large scale a true calamity in its consequences, destined to be stupid – almost as stupid as if trying to abolish bad weather – say from pity for the poor... In the overall system, the calamities of reality (in its effects, in desires, in the will to power) are to an incalculable measure more important than that form of petty happiness which people call 'goodness'. You actually have to be quite forbearing to the latter to give it some space, since it is based on instinctive falseness. I will find a major occasion to demonstrate how the historical consequences of *optimism*, this spawn of great men, have been sinister beyond belief. Zarathustra, who was the first to grasp that the optimist is just as decadent as the pessimist, and perhaps more harmful, says, *'Good men never speak the truth. Treacherous coastlines and assurances have been taught to you by the good; in the lies of the good you were hatched and huddled. Everything is riddled through and through with, and twisted by, the lies of the good.'*

Luckily, the world has not been built on such instincts that only good-natured herd animals may find their narrow happiness in it, to demand that all should become 'good men', herd animals, blue-eyed, complaisant, 'beautiful souls' – or, as Mr Herbert Spencer would have it, altruistic – that would deprive existence of its *great* character and would castrate humanity and reduce us all to a stagnant state of misery.

And they have tried to! Precisely this they called morality… In this sense, Zarathustra calls the good now 'the last men', now the 'beginning of the end'; above all, he considers this type of man the most harmful, because they enforce their existence at the expense of *truth* as well as at the expense of the *future*.

' – The good – are unable to *create*; they are always the beginning of the end;

– they crucify him who writes *new* values on new tablets; they sacrifice the future to themselves; they crucify the future of all of man!

– The good – have always been the beginning of the end…

– And whatever harm those who sling mud at the world may do, *the harm done by the good is the most harmful harm.*'

5.

ZARATHUSTRA, the first psychologist of the good, is therefore a friend of the wicked. When a decadent type of man has risen to the rank of finest character, this could only happen at the expense of its counterpart, the strong and self-confident type. When the herd animal radiates purest virtue, the exceptional man must have been reduced to the level of the wicked. If falseness monopolizes the word 'truth' at any price, the really truthful man is bound to be branded with the worst names. Zarathustra leaves no doubt here: he says that it had been precisely the perception of the good, 'the very best' that made him shudder at the sight of man in general; from *this* dislike he had grown his wings, 'to soar off into distant futures' – he does not conceal the fact that *his* type of man, a relatively superhuman type, is superhuman precisely in relation to the *good* – that the good and just would call his superman *the devil.*

'You men of highest rank whom my eyes looked upon, this is my doubt in you and my secret mirth: I assume you would call my superman: the devil! You are so estranged in your soul from all that is great that superman would be terrifying to you in his goodness.' It is at this point and nowhere else that you must make a start to grasp what Zarathustra wants: this type of man of his own conception, conceives reality *as it is*: it is strong enough for that – this type is not estranged or removed from reality, it is reality *itself* and exemplifies all that is terrible and questionable in it – *only in that way can man attain greatness...*

6.

BUT HERE is yet another sense in which I have chosen the word *immoralist* for myself as a symbol and badge of honour; I am proud of knowing this word that sets me apart from all of humanity. Nobody has as yet felt *Christian* morality to be *beneath* him: for this you need great height, a farsightedness, a hitherto unheard of psychological depth and profundity. Christian morality has until now been the femme fatale to all thinkers – they were in her service.

Who has entered before me the lairs from which the poisonous stench of this type of ideal (of world slandering) rises? Who even dared to suspect that these are lairs in the first place? Who among philosophers was actually a *psychologist* before me and not rather the opposite, a 'superior swindler' and 'idealist'? There was no psychology at all before me. To be the first here can also be a curse – it is at all events a destiny: *for you are also the first to despise…* The *distaste* for mankind is my danger…

7.

DID YOU GET MY MEANING?

What defines me and sets me apart from the rest of humanity is the fact that I *exposed* Christian morality. That is why I needed a word that would be a challenge to everyone. The fact that they did not open their eyes earlier at this point is to me the greatest stain on man's conscience; it is a self-deception that has become instinct, that is a fundamental principle *to close* their eyes to everything that happens, to every causality, to every reality, as psychological fraudulence that borders on criminality. Blindness to Christianity is the *absolute crime* – the crime *against life*…

Thousands of years have passed and all people, the first and the last, the philosophers and the old women, they are all as bad as each other as far as this matter is concerned – apart from five or six moments in history (I am the seventh). The Christian has so far been *the* 'moral being', a rare curiosity and, *as* the 'moral being' more absurd, false, vain, frivolous and *acting more to his own disadvantage* than even the greatest rejecter of mankind could dream up. Christian morality, the most malignant form of the will to lie, the true femme fatale of mankind, corrupted it. It is *not* the error as such which horrifies me when I look at this fact, *not* the lack of 'good will' for two millennia, of discipline, of decency, of spiritual courage, revealed by its victory – it is the lack of naturalness and the utterly horrific fact that *perversion* itself received the highest honours as morality and was left to govern humanity as law and categorical imperative… To fail to such an extent – *not* as individuals, *not* as people, but as humanity!… That they taught us to despise the primary instincts of life, that they made up a 'soul' and a 'spirit' to abuse the body, that they taught us to find something unclean in the precondition for life – sexuality; that even in the most profound quality for any growth, strict self-interest (even the word is pejorative!), they seek the evil principle, and that, conversely, they regard the *higher* value, what am I saying, the *absolute* value, in the typical signs of decline and contradictory instincts, that is to say in 'selflessness', in loss of gravity, in 'depersonalization' and 'charity' (addictive charity!)… What? Is humanity itself decadent? Was it always?

One thing is certain, that it has been *taught* only decadent values as supreme values. The losing of the Self-morality is the absolute morality of decline, the fact 'I am losing myself' has been translated into the imperative 'you must all lose yourself' – and *not just* into the imperative!... The only morality that has been taught so far is to lose your Self and it reveals a will to end all – it is a basic negation of life.

This could leave open the possibility that humanity is not degenerating, but only that type of parasitic man, the *priest*, who with lies and deceptions about morality became the definer of values – who divined that Christian morality would be his means to *power*... And indeed, *this* is my discovery: the teachers, the leaders of mankind, theologians all of them, were also Decadents on the whole: *hence* the re-evaluation of all values into hostility to life, *hence* morality... *definition of morality*: morality – the idiosyncrasy of Decadents with the hidden agenda to take revenge on life – successfully. I find this definition very important.

8.

DID YOU GET MY MEANING?

Everything I have just said, I said five years ago with Zarathustra as my mouthpiece. The *uncovering* of Christian morality is an event unparalleled, a true catastrophe. He who enlightens the world about it is a *force majeure*, a destiny – he breaks the history of mankind in two. You live *before* him or you live *after* him.

The lightning bolt of truth struck precisely that which was held in highest esteem: whoever understands *what* has been destroyed may look down on his hands to see whether he still has something left to hold. All that was called 'truth' up to now has been recognized as the most harmful, insidious and underhand form of lie: the sacred pretext of 'improving' humanity as an uncanny attempt to *suck* the blood of life itself – morality as *vampirism*...

Whoever uncovers morality also discovers the lack of value in all values in which we believe or have believed. He no longer sees anything venerable in the most venerated, even *canonized* type of man. He sees the most fatal type of crippled existence in them, fatal because they fascinate...

The concept of 'God', invented as an anti-climax to life, stands for all that is harmful, poisonous, slandering and the deathly hostility against life in one dreadful unity. The concept of 'other world' or 'better world' was invented to devalue the *only* world in existence, in order not to keep a single aim, reason or task for our earthly reality. The concept of our 'soul', 'spirit' and finally even 'immortal soul' were invented to make us despise our body, to render it sick, 'holy', to meet all things that deserve to be taken seriously: the questions of nourishment, accommodation, education, nursing care, hygiene and weather, with dreadful flippancy! Instead of health the idea of 'salvation of the soul' (a folly wedged between pathological use of penitence and redemption-hysteria of manic depressive intensity) was invented together with the associated instrument of torture, the concept of 'free will', to confuse the instincts that make mistrust of our instincts second nature. The concept of the 'selfless' and 'self-denial' are the defining signs of decadence; the *attraction* of the harmful, the *inability* to evaluate your own usefulness and self-destruction were turned into proof of value itself, into 'duty', into 'holiness', into what is 'divine' in man! Finally, and this is the most terrible, the concept of the *good* man takes the side of all that is weak, sick, misshapen and suffering, of all those that ought to perish – the law of selection is crossed and an ideal born out of opposition to those proud and well-made, those who say 'Yes', those who are sure of the future, who safeguard the future – this is now called *evil*... And all this was believed and called *morality*! *Ecrasez l'infâme!*

9.

DID YOU GET MY MEANING? – *Dionysus versus the man on the Cross.*